An Introduction To
EGYPTIAN ART

An Introduction To
EGYPTIAN ART

Boris de Rachewiltz

Translated by R. H. Boothroyd

SPRING BOOKS · LONDON

Originally published in Italy under
the title *Incontro con l' Arte Egiziana*
by Aldo Martello Editore, Milan.
First published in Great Britain 1960 by
Hutchinson & Co., Ltd.

English translation
© Copyright Hutchinson & Co., Ltd, 1960
This edition published 1966 by Spring Books
Drury House · Russell Street · London WC2

Second Impression 1967

Printed in Great Britain by
Fletcher & Son Ltd, Norwich
and bound by Richard Clay
(The Chaucer Press) Ltd, Bungay, Suffolk

FOR
MARY

For their help in collecting the material for this volume the author wishes to express his sincere thanks to Professor Ahmed Badawi, director of the Centre de documentation et d'études sur l'histoire de l'art et de la civilization de l'ancienne Égypte; Dr. M. Kamal, director of the Cairo Museum; Professor Selim Hassan and Professor Abdel Kader Rizk of the Department of Fine Arts in the Ministry of Public Education at Cairo; the late Zakaria Goneim, formerly Chief Inspector of the necropolis in Sakkâra; Professors H. Ricke and H. Stock of the Swiss-German Archaeological Mission for permission to reproduce the 'royal head' found during the excavations at Abusir; Professor E. Scamuzzi, director of the museum in Turin; Mr. I. E. S. Edwards, M.A., Keeper of Egyptian Antiquities at the British Museum; and Madame Güner H. Elgen for valuable help with the photographs.

CONTENTS

ILLUSTRATIONS

In colour

9

In black and white

10

15

17

FOREWORD

Much has been written and is still being written about the intriguing art of the Egypt of the Pharaohs: sumptuous tomes full of stupendous photographs follow one upon another, aesthetical theories clash and contradict each other, and libraries are filled with weighty volumes to such an extent that one is entitled to ask whether any further books on this subject are justified.

The aim which the author has set himself in writing the following pages—or at all events his intention—differs from that of the usual publications. These, by means of careful subdivisions of chronology and material, offer the reader a 'history of art' rather than a spiritual approach to a world from which we are separated, not only by several thousands of years, but by a different mentality, a completely different conception of life.

Is it possible to build a bridge between the two worlds of ancient Egypt and today, or is there any object in trying to do so?

In attempting to answer this question, and at the same time to avoid producing a mere 'catalogue' of Egyptian art accompanied by a commentary, I have not merely followed the chronological order in the treatment of the material, but have subordinated it to the development of 'ideas'. If necessary, elements posterior in date are mentioned side by side with those of earlier epochs, but this does not mean that the treatment is fragmentary. Everything, including elements which are apparently quite disparate, is arranged according to a pre-established guiding thread.

In the history of the human race Egypt occupies a place of its own. Almost disdainful, enclosed within the circle of its conceptions which are as mysterious as the language in which they are expressed, she does not easily yield to the first comer. The phenomenon of 'art' is one of the principal manifestations of her existence and is a tangible demonstration of the philosophical conceptions that characterized her civilization for three thousand years.

The study of Egyptian 'art' is thus a means of penetrating into the world which gave birth to it, an adventure which will not be without its surprises and unexpected encounters. A close examination of unconfutable elements may well lead to the demolition of preconceptions and superficial opinions based on commonplaces or on ridiculous arbitrary reconstructions. That in itself would be sufficient to 'justify' the present volume. But if it should also result in an intuition of a 'something' which, in the world of ideas, unites the past with the present and the future, and of which Egyptian art is a fleeting gleam, then the author will feel that he has achieved his aim.

B. de R.

EGYPTIAN ART

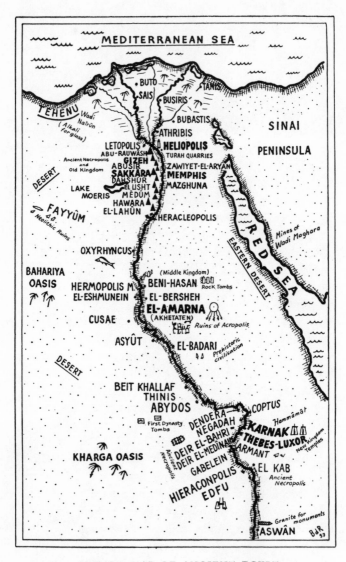

SKETCH MAP OF ANCIENT EGYPT

CHAPTER ONE

Definition of the boundaries

WHEN we try to understand the essence of Egyptian art, we find ourselves face to face with a civilization which, after thousands of years of prehistory, suddenly made its appearance in an already mature form, with hardly any of the usual signs of infancy.

To what strange miracle must we ascribe the fact that even in the days of the First Dynasty those schemes appear which were to remain the classic models for another three thousand years? How are we to explain the absence of any fundamental evolution —in the modern sense of the term—in Egyptian art? Why is it characterized by an exotic and hieratical flavour which compels us to adopt a different mental attitude towards it and a system of valuation different from that which we use when considering, for example, the Apollo Belvedere?

To find answers to these questions is the chief aim of the present study, and this brings us into direct contact with the intimate psychology of the ancient inhabitants of the Nile Valley and with the rules which governed their 'artistic production'. This is a debatable term, since the idea of art for art's sake, of a light-hearted search for beauty for the sake of artistic enjoyment, was completely foreign to the mental processes of the ancient Egyptians. No other civilization had as its fundamental characteristic, raised to the level of an affair of State, the struggle against death. It was this concept, either expressed or latent, that permeated the fundamental aspects of the life of the Egyptian people, governing all their institutions and rites. For them, immortality was not acquired *de jure* at birth, but was a conquest—and by no means an easy one—subordinated to definite rules. 'To become immortal' meant being able to participate in the very essence of divinity, to insert one's own individual *ego* into the eternal cycle of creation, freeing it from the laws of the future; such, in substance, was the aim of the funerary rites based on magic. But the achievement of this aim was subordinated to the faculty of 'appropriating' the very natural laws used by the Demiurge in his work of creation.

The Pythagorean axiom that 'God works everywhere by means of geometry' is a good way of expressing the result of these musings of the ancient Egyptians, who, being close observers of Nature, had noticed the persistence of identical laws in the macrocosm and in the microcosm, in the harmonious movement of the stars, in man, in even the smallest insects, in the web spun by a spider, in the petal of a flower. Laws of harmony, laws of a sublime mathematics, which determine the very structure of living beings throughout the biological hierarchy. And thousands of years before Leonardo Fibonaci of Pisa they had divined those geometrical relationships such as the 'golden section' which govern the universe. It is for this reason that the Rhind papyrus begins with the statement: 'Exact calculation: the gateway leading to all things.' Numbers were thus the very key to 'knowledge' and governed all artistic creation. E. C. Kielland's analysis of this kind of production from the First Dynasty onwards, for example in the palette of King Narmer (Plate 1), shows the integral application of geometrical rules, in other words the obedience to a 'canon', which, as J. Capart also points out, became an absolutely valid norm in all subsequent artistic activity. This 'canon' and its strict application inevitably led to a restriction of the artist's freedom of expression, confining it to pre-established schemes governed by mathematical calculations. A gesture, an attitude, an arm raised at a particular angle, are thus reproduced, not because the artist wished to give free rein to his own feelings or vision, but because the preceding geometrical calculation which constituted the solution of the spatial problem—a problem of relationships—established the co-ordinates and abscissae, the 'points of intersection' of the various elements forming the composition. Nor was that all. The functionality of Egyptian art, that is to say the finalistic conception of the artificial 'creation' of immortality, was governed by magico-religious rules implying a limitation of the field in which the artist's imagination could hover, and it was this finalism that, as regards general trend, distinguished it from Greek art, in which aesthetic 'canons' also existed: in the case of Egyptian art one might even say that it was an art conditioned by death.

Tombs, which offer us an epitome of all artistic activity, were decorated with scenes from the everyday life of the owner, graded according to his rank and profession. For the most part they are agricultural scenes, or else they show craftsmen at work or banquets with the inevitable accompaniment of music and dancing, in all the nuances found in real life, so that the *Ka* of the deceased, that is to say his 'double' or astral body, when shut up in the 'eternal abode', might continue to enjoy an ephemeral existence throughout the centuries. But only if the scenes represented conformed with the mathematical and geometrical rules, if, that is to say, a definite relationship had been created between the plane of the 'absolute' and that of the 'concrete', could the scenes in question be animated by the voice of the officiating priest, the *kheri-heb* or lector-priest, on the day when the tomb was sealed. This was obviously a legacy from prehistoric times, when the nomad hunters of the Nile Valley, with magical intent, reproduced on rocks and the walls of tombs the figures of the animals they intended to hunt. Like their predecessors or contemporaries in other lands who indulged in rock-carving, they believed that the 'object' represented had an intimate connexion with the corresponding reality and that it was therefore possible to influence the latter by depicting it. This is, in substance, the conception governing the practice of *envoûtement* which has survived down to our own days. Naturally, the more lifelike the representation, the greater the magical effect.

The Egyptians, as they perfected their technique, tended—by idealizing the forms—towards the creation of archetypes which, in obedience to the laws of a superior harmony, the same laws that governed all

26

things created, inserted the dynamic individualizing force of the Cosmos into the empty receptacle of a silhouette. This is the basis of the realism of the ideogrammatic pictography expressed by hieroglyphs. In their highest form these represented 'reality' down to the minutest detail: colour, if it was a question of painting, the plumage of birds—everything was expressed and enclosed within the elegant drawing. The magical value lay in the identification with the 'reality', and it was for this reason that after the ritual reading of texts, signs were hammered on to the walls of tombs which—though they necessarily had phonetic values—represented on the plane of reality dangerous animals which might imperil the existence of the *Ka*. They were hammered on or else attached by transfixing them with daggers, as is the case with the serpent in the tomb of Kheruef at Thebes, here reproduced (Plate 3) together with the hieroglyphs surrounding it, in order to give an adequate idea of the decorative value of Egyptian writing.

To the same order of ideas belongs the series of discs, described as being 'of unknown use', from the First Dynasty tomb of Hemaka (Plates A and B). The reader should note the close similarity between these and the circle enclosing the animals in the centre of a pre-dynastic mural painting (Plate 2). The operative mechanism is the same: it is a question of creating, by means of magical praxis, the ideal conditions for successful hunting. Whether the circle itself is a highly esteemed magical formula, or whether it symbolizes a trap, is of no great importance. The crux of the question lies in the possibility of predetermining an action by depicting the beings against whom the action is to be directed. The Hemaka discs were provided with holes so that they could be rotated on a pivot. In this way the scene acquired movement: the dogs appeared to be pursuing and biting their prey, which was substantially the aim of hunting. The discs were thus a kind of magical spinning-top, for the vertiginous dynamism imparted by the operator produced an abstract version of the pre-ordained sequence, which, like a seed sown on fertile soil, would bear fruit on the plane of reality. The same can be said of the disc showing captive birds, and in this case the lozenges round the edge might represent a net, the empty space in the middle of the lozenge symbolizing the interstices between the meshes. This hypothesis finds support in the representation, on another of these discs, of a typical trap for birds.

All these conceptions, which germinated during the dark centuries of the prehistoric period, influenced the creation of the statues of deceased persons placed in the appropriate recess, the *serdab*, and the statues of the gods jealously preserved in the 'holy of holies' of temples.

The sculptor, or *sankh*, was the man who, as his name implies, 'gave life', since statues, according to the most ancient traditions of Memphis, could harbour the manifestations of the Demiurge.

Here, however, the artist enjoyed a certain amount of liberty, owing to the religious conceptions forming the basis of statuary. These, in fact, laid down that the portrait should reproduce as faithfully as possible the actual features of the deceased, so that the respective

Ka might recognize the image reproduced and would not have to wander about the necropolis in a vain search for its own abiding-place. This explains the contemporaneous presence, in one and the same tomb, of several statues of the deceased, so that, if some of them were to be destroyed, at least one would remain (this, at all events, was the hope) to carry out its proper function.

The same rule, religious and at the same time aesthetic, applied to the statues of private individuals and, *a fortiori*, to those of sovereigns: apart from the pose of the body, which crystallized into ritual attitudes, the constant variation of the features has resulted in the preservation of what are occasionally real masterpieces. It should, however, be noted at this point that, notwithstanding the difference of features characterizing individuals, there existed a common denominator, namely the complete absence of all signs of emotion and of details specifying human feelings and passions. These images invariably have an almost aloof tone, a 'bland beatitude', as if they no longer participate in the life of this world, and, in addition, a tone of extreme dignity, almost of a higher existence which has been achieved and of which the subject is completely aware. We shall see later how this effect was achieved.

The creation of 'masterpieces' would seem to be in contradiction with what we have just said. But this is not the case. Even if no concept of 'art for art's sake' existed, this did not necessarily imply that no 'works of art' existed. The bison of Altamira, a product of remote Magdalenian rock-painting, is certainly a masterpiece which excites our aesthetic admiration, however conscious we may be of the fact that the artist who created it was thinking of something very different from arousing the admiration of his contemporaries or handing down a work of art to posterity. The same rule applies to the artistic productions of ancient Egypt and explains why we admire certain works without paying any heed to the reasons which were the basis of their creation.

In tombs, as we have already said, it was the custom to place several statues of the deceased, each differing from the others. The difference was not only a matter of clothing, but also of the features themselves. According to J. Capart, this was an 'idealization', a desire to 'beautify' that which was not beautiful. He maintains that Old Kingdom statues represent only men and women in their prime, without any trace of old age. Anxious to please their clients, the sculptors—according to the same author—made their works conform to the ideal of physical beauty prevalent at the time.

That is not quite correct and is in contradiction with the concept we have already mentioned, which governed, allowing for the necessary realism, all the production of funerary statues. Take, among many other examples, the Third Dynasty statue of King Zoser found in the *serdab* of the step pyramid at Sakkâra, which is a realistic rendering of the sovereign, already advanced in years and undermined by disease (Plate 4), in striking contrast to the youthful portrait (Plate 9) on a bas-relief in his tomb. Observe, too, the crude realism of the dwarf Seneb and his family

(Plate 5), and the adipose standing figure dating from a later period (Plate 6). We certainly cannot speak of any 'idealization' of beauty!

In the course of the excavations carried out by the University of Alexandria in the Old Kingdom necropolis at Gizeh, Professor Abu Bakr found in a tomb two statues of the owner: in one of these the deceased is represented in her prime, glowing with youth; in the other she is shown at the time of her death, old and realistically ugly, but still recognizable.

Apart from the realism, in this particular branch of statuary in which the artist really has a chance to show his skill, the adherence to the 'canon' and to the finalistic conception inevitably led to the creation of a series of standard models and motives which are repeated, not without a certain monotony, in the sepulchral bas-reliefs. And in fact this was bound to be so, because, as we have already said, it was a question of real and proper 'archetypes', which, according to Egyptian ideas, 'vibrated' on the same plane on which it was supposed that the *Ka* existed, allowing the latter to enjoy a sensorial participation in their lives.

The social structure of the old Pharaonic state also had considerable influence on artistic production. In the theocratic state, the control of culture was exercised from the recesses of the temples. Sculpture was not a 'free profession'; if we exclude a few rare exceptions at the time of Akhenaten, there were no workshops run by individual artists, and as a rule the work was collective and anonymous.

To be an 'artist', it was necessary to have a technical

mastery of the instruments and a knowledge of the 'canon'; in all other respects, an ability to copy standard models was sufficient. The word denoting art, *hemwt*, had no abstract meaning; its determinative sign was the drill used by stonemasons.

One artist, on a stele now in the Louvre, has tried to synthesize his ability: 'I know the pose for the statue of a man walking and the line of the statue of a woman, the pose of the vulture, that of a spear at the moment in which it strikes an adversary, the way in which people look at one another, the expression of terror on the face of a captive enemy, the way in which a hunter raises his arm as he strikes a hippopotamus, the poise of a running man.'

This explains clearly why identical motives were repeated after an interval of thousands of years: the attitude of King Udimu of the First Dynasty in the act of slaying an enemy, as reproduced on the ivory plaque in the McGregor collection, is the same as that of Tuthmosis III on the pillars of the temple at Karnak. Undoubtedly individual artists, though still adhering to the rules of the 'canon' and keeping within the limits prescribed by the theme, sometimes evolved new models, such as a crocodile being devoured by a hippopotamus in a pool or a cow weeping for the milk of which its calf has been deprived (Plate 7); but these 'whiffs of fresh air' are superimposed on the already existing themes, and it was not long before they too became standardized forms, repeated to the point of boredom.

Nor was there any lack of attempts to create 'pure forms'. A typical example is the plate, also from the

32

PLATE 1. Verso of the palette of King Narmer. Slate. From Hieraconpolis.
Height 25¼ inches; 64 cm. *Cairo, Museum.*

PLATE 2. Detail of a painting in a predynastic tomb. From Hieraconpolis.
(Note the animals and the circle in the centre.)

PLATE 3. Specimen of hieroglyphic writing. Eighteenth Dynasty.
Tomb of Kheruef, Thebes.

PLATE 4. Detail of statue of King Zoser. Painted limestone. From Sakkâra.
Third Dynasty. Original 55 inches high. *Cairo, Museum.*

PLATE 5. The dwarf Seneb and his family. Group in painted limestone. From Gizeh. Sixth Dynasty. Original 13 inches high; 33 cm. *Cairo, Museum.*

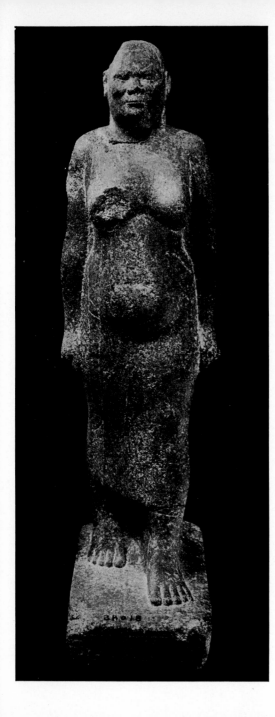

PLATE 6. Portrait of Prince Arigadiganen. Grey granite. Saitic period. Height of original 17¾ inches; 45 cm. *Cairo, Museum.*

PLATE 7. "The Weeping Cow". From the sarcophagus of Queen Kawit. Eleventh Dynasty. *Cairo, Museum*.

PLATE 8. "Plate" made of slate, from the tomb of the Vizier Hemaka in Sakkâra. First Dynasty. Diameter about $23\frac{1}{2}$ inches; 60 cm. *Cairo, Museum.*

PLATE 9. Bas-relief of King Zoser. Third Dynasty. From his tomb at Sakkâra.
(Note the network traced in ink on the background.)

PLATE 10. Detail of one of the wooden panels of Hesire. Third Dynasty.
Height of whole panel 45¼ inches; 115 cm. *Cairo, Museum.*

PLATE 11. Sculptors at work. From the tomb of Kaemrehu at Sakkâra.
Sixth Dynasty. *Cairo, Museum.*

PLATE 12. Sculptors' studies. Preliminary phase. From Sakkâra. New Kingdom.
Height of originals about 8¼ inches; 21 cm. *Cairo, Museum.*

PLATE 13. "Cubic" statue of Senmut with the little Princess Neferure. Black granite. Eighteenth Dynasty. Height about 34 inches; 86 cm. *Cairo, Museum.*

PLATE 14. "Famine". Bas-relief from the "sacred way" of King Unis at Sakkâra, Fifth Dynasty.

PLATE 15. Details from the "Battle". Bas-reliefs from the "sacred way" of King Unis at Sakkâra. Fifth Dynasty.

PLATE 16. Archaic ivory statuette of a sovereign wearing the crown of Upper Egypt. From Abydos. Height 3½ inches; 8.8 cm. *London, British Museum.*

PLATE 17. Fragment of a painted limestone bas-relief. King Snefru and a divinity with a feline head. Fourth Dynasty. *Dahshûr.*

PLATE 18. Ivory statuette of King Cheops. Fourth Dynasty. Height of original about 2 inches; 5 cm. *Cairo, Museum.*

tomb of Hemaka and described as being 'of unknown use' (Plate 8). Out of the slate, a hard material liable to splinter, the artist, as if he were working with plastic clay, has managed to create harmonious lines, 'non-utilitarian' in appearance, but, in the simplicity of its synthesis, a source of aesthetic enjoyment.

Once we have accepted as principle the adaptation of artistic production to a 'canon' considered as an expression of the divine law of harmony, any evolution in a dynamic direction becomes a departure from truth, and thus, in substance, a regression.

That is the basic reason of the static character of Egyptian art.

The revolution brought about in the field of the arts, as well as in other things, by the schism of Akhenaten, limited to that period alone, merits special attention, which we shall give it in due course. The influence of fashion, or of contingent mani-festations and trends in certain periods, does not alter the fundamental unitary value of Pharaonic art, conditioned, as we have seen, by its finality and by its subordination to rules which remained essentially unchanged for three thousand years. Must we, for this reason, deny the existence of new trends in form or the presence, in the midst of that civilization, of outstanding artistic personalities? Certainly not. During all periods, and even under the most rigid discipline, personalities assert themselves which, in defiance of the rules imposed by that discipline, give a special character even to their own times. Men like Imhotep, the creator of the step pyramid—a milestone in Egyptian architecture—who was even ranked among the deities of that Olympus; the architects Hapuseneb, Ineni and Senmut; the sculptors Bek, Tuthmosis—who bequeathed to us the legacy of his workshop—and Iuty during the reign of Akhenaten; the painter Nebamun at Thebes under the Eighteenth Dynasty—all these can be considered as outstanding personalities in the history of Egyptian art. But that does not detract anything from, or add anything to, what we have said. The art of this civilization remains an anonymous product of the royal and temple workshops, linked with a finalistic conception and subordinated to the laws of mathematical calculation.

The realistic images produced by sculptors were partially exempted from these laws, as were also, though not in an absolute sense owing to the persistent application of geometrical rules, the minor arts, the products of craftsmen which will also be included in our survey. But before examining the products of individual branches of art, we must first make a brief pause, in order to study the conception of the 'canon' and the rules which governed this production.

CHAPTER TWO

Artistic creation

INSTEAD of considering the rules governing artistic production from the purely theoretical standpoint, it will be better if we study their practical application, taking as our basis the surviving documentary proofs of the various phases of creation. On the walls of a great number of tombs dating from the oldest periods, e.g. the Third Dynasty tomb of Zoser, we find, traced in ink, vertical and horizontal lines intersecting so as to form a ground, a grid divided into regular quadrangles (Plate 9). The implication of this is that drawings previously made to scale on the 'cartoons' of the period were subsequently 'transferred' to the walls. Sometimes the scale is varied, larger proportions being used for the more important figures and vice versa; but these are technical details which do not in any way affect the principle. In other tombs there are tracings, likewise in ink, of human figures, traversed by lines of red dots to mark the planned sections, and not infrequently the traced drawing is followed by a partial engraving of the figure—this being the first step towards the execution of the bas-relief. The same procedure is found in statuary. Together with completely finished series of statues, we may find one which is only in the rough, showing traces of ink at the points that had still to be hewn. It is generally believed that tombs containing such relics of technique are 'unfinished' tombs, work on which was suspended owing to the sudden death of the owner. This statement, however, is too superficial, not only because the number of such tombs is very considerable, but also, and above all, because it contrasts with the idea rooted in the souls of the Egyptians and reduced to a code of rules, namely the idea of making provision for one's tomb in good time while still alive. In the *Maxims* of Ani we read: 'Build for thyself a fine abode in the Valley of the Desert, in the recesses whereof thou canst hide thy body. Remember this amidst all thy occupations, as did thy great ancestors, who rest in their sepulchres. He who does this will not incur the divine wrath. . . .'

The fact that evidence of incompleteness has been found even in the tombs of sovereigns is a too-glaring contradiction of this doctrine, all the more so since the Pharaoh should have been the first to think of preparing his own 'abode for all eternity'. An explanation—or at least a hypothesis—of the reason for this practice might be that, although the Egyptians were interested in providing every possible comfort in their tombs during their own lifetime, they were in no particular hurry to inhabit them; in fact, one of the sacramental texts that the owners caused to be incised on their tombs was the following: 'May the King approve and grant that he [the proprietor] be buried in the necropolis of the western cemetery, after reaching an advanced age. . . .' To return to what we have said regarding the value of the scenes represented in tombs, the fact that they were often left unfinished was in all probability due to some kind of magical praxis designed to postpone until as late as possible the day of death. Once the execution of the various scenes had been completely finished, the tomb was ready to receive its owner, whereas 'incompleteness' put off the event until a 'tomorrow' (i.e. the moment when all the representations had been finished). We shall return to this subject later on.

Be that as it may, and quite apart from the reasons for the practice, the fact remains, and it is a valuable aid for us in our study of the technical process of execution.

A century ago Lepsius formulated his 'canon' derived from his study of unfinished designs in tombs at Sakkâra and founded on the assumption that the basic unit for the proportions of the figures and of the grid forming the background was the dimensions of the feet of the figures. It would seem, however, that this canon was not always respected, and other scholars, e.g. Edgar, Marcelle Baud, Perrot and Chipiez, extended the study of this field to observations and investigations which it is unnecessary for us to consider here, until Lange elaborated his celebrated 'Law of Frontality' which, constituting as it does one of the main pillars of modern aesthetic criticism of Egyptian art, we reproduce below:

The following rules are applicable to statues in primitive art. They reproduced the body in all kinds of poses: walking, standing still, erect, bending forward or backward, seated on a chair or on the ground, on horseback, kneeling, lying on the back or on the stomach, etc., but whatever the pose assumed by the figure, it was subjected to the following rule: The median plane, which may be considered as passing through the top of the head, the nose, the spinal column, the breast-bone, the navel and the genital organs, dividing the body into two symmetrical parts, remains invariable and may not be bent or curved in either direction. A figure may thus bend forward or backward, but this does not mean that the median plane ceases to be a plane, and there is no lateral flexion or torsion either of the neck or of the torso. . . .

Lange calls the pose of the figures 'frontal', a term which has become classic.

His theory has been subjected to close scrutiny, especially by H. Schäfer, who formulated the law of three-dimensional sculpture:

The carved figures of human beings and animals, in the case of all countries and all individual artists not influenced by Greek art of the fifth century B.C., are subjected to a law which is a consequence of the concordance between the frontal vision and the nature of the body of the human being according to the circumstances; a primary plane is conceived as being seen frontally, and all the other main vertical planes of the trunk and limbs form with it an intersection of perpendicular contiguous or parallel planes. This rule is applied both to single figures and to groups conceived as a sculptural unity. The figures are in harmonious juxtaposition, whether they are on the same plane or at right-angles to one another. . . .

An intimate relationship is thus created between the work of sculpture and its projection on a plane, in the case of bas-reliefs. This relationship is the basis of the typical representations of the human figure seen in profile with frontal projection of the eye and shoulders, which, as regards the median horizontal axis of the body, seem to have been subjected to a distortion without, however, any impression of effort. Take, for example, one of the famous Third Dynasty reliefs of Hesirē' (Plate 10), executed on a wooden panel. The classic automaton-like pose obeys the strict rules of geometrical calculation. The masterly execution becomes clear when we note the minute care with which the features have been treated, the undulations of the wig indicated by horizontal grooves, and lastly the balanced harmony of the masses. All this shows that, even as early as the Third Dynasty, this type of 'art' had reached the apex of its possibilities. It is a typical example of the representation of the human figure in the manner described above.

The hypothesis advanced by some writers as to the reasons for this manner of representation, allegedly due to an inability on the part of the Egyptians to work in any other way—almost as if they were bound to primitive forms which excluded all other possibilities—collapses when we confront it with documentary evidence. I would refer the reader to the scene showing craftsmen working on two statues (Plate 11). Here, while the actual personages are shown in the typical projection, the statues are presented in perfect profile, clearly proving the 'ability' to represent reality under this aspect as well. Nor is this an isolated instance; there are numerous examples of this type.

The choice of this characteristic method of representing the human figure must therefore have been deliberate. In this we might see an attempt to resolve the problem of 'space-time' in bas-reliefs. On a flat surface ('space') an image is drawn which at the same moment ('time') evokes a plurality of individual visions. It is almost as if the figure were visualized from several sides, seen simultaneously in profile and from the front in its essential 'reality', which is derived from one vision of the various sides synthesized on the flat surface. No detail which can in any way serve to create this impression is neglected, and on the other hand every accidental element is discarded.

To that we must add another observation. A bas-relief representing the deceased was in every respect a substitute for a 'statue' of him. In front of such reliefs, the *sem*—the priest entrusted with the performance of such ceremonies—celebrated the rites of vivification in order to establish a link of co-relationship between the *Ka* of the deceased and the carved or painted scenes.

It is thus in the idea of a statue 'projected' on to a flat surface that we must seek the motive of this technique of representation. Once again the 'finalistic' conception is manifested through its laws.

Let us now analyse the successive phases of the sculptural 'experience'. The block of stone was first squared so as to provide sufficiently smooth surfaces. On the front and side forming a right-angle the outline of the subject was then traced in ink. Subsequently, by incising the tracing on the two planes, the point of contact was reached which constituted the first rough draft of the statue. This contained

only the 'essentials' of the form: there was no speci-
fication going beyond a synthesis of the chief lines.
It was, of course, possible to see whether the personage were standing or seated, whether it was the
figure of a divinity or a *naophorous* statue, but there
was no attempt to go beyond the 'Platonic' conception of the subject (Plate 12).

Elaborating this, the craftsman began to specify
the details: the vertical and horizontal planes, intersecting one another, produced a series of 'cubic'
forms; this was a tangible geometry of masses, no
longer an abstraction, but visible reality. The experiment, which we might describe as 'cubistic',
although in itself it was but a stage on the path
towards the definite execution of the work, resulted
in a particular type of statuary in which the separate
elements were fused in the pure geometrical form.
Generally the subjects were personages of high rank,
depicted in a characteristic attitude, seated on the
ground with their arms crossed above the knees. Only
the head was given adequate treatment and seems, at a
first glance, to be emerging from a cube. Take, for
example, the Eighteenth Dynasty version of Senmut
with the Princess Neferurē' in the museum at Cairo
(Plate 13). There is no trace of the limbs; everything
is fused into a geometrical form, including the synthetic rendering of the feet, while the flat surface is
utilized for the inscription of a hieroglyphic text.
This is a complete abstraction of forms, whereby,
more than in other cases, Egyptian sculpture could
be reduced to a mere system of co-ordinates.

41

CHAPTER THREE

Finalism and Narrative

THE scenes represented in tombs depict, as we have
said, 'episodes from life' typical of ancient Egypt—
agriculture, hunting, banquets, etc. Some writers
speak of 'archetypes', which—by virtue of some
magical praxis—are supposed to comprise the dynamic
individualizing force of the Cosmos. But after deeper
analysis, when it is affirmed that the basis of such
representations is the desire—on the part of the
deceased's *Ka*—to continue the life he led in this
world, we are compelled to examine this term more
closely. The term in itself is dynamic, not a static
documentation of acts performed in the past, but an
active functionality projected into the future. Once
the scenes had been animated, in their ritual conception, by the appropriate formulae, they began to
lead their own lives, which cannot be conceived
otherwise than as a succession of dynamic acts.
What different explanation can be given, among the
many others, of the scenes depicting the hunting of
birds, in which all the phases, both antecedent and
subsequent, are expressed contemporaneously in the
pictorial representation? One could compare such
scenes with a musical score, of which only the deceased
possesses the instrument necessary for playing it. He
can choose at any moment the passage which he
prefers; potentially the whole ensemble of the scenes

is alive, but the separate parts composing it are brought to life at the moment desired.

They are not, however, narrative or biographical scenes, nor are they concerned with the conveying of any message from the artist to the spectator: in substance, they constitute a series of 'typical acts'.

In such scenes the deceased is usually depicted in a passive state, as a spectator of what is going on around him. Seated on his stool, he confines himself to receiving in an almost automatic fashion the funerary offerings or tributes brought to him by the representatives of his domains; or else he makes a tour of inspection in a boat, enjoying the music and dancing in the company of his guests. This rôle of spectator, however, means that he is extraneous to the life of the composition at least as regards any direct participation in it, almost as if, to put it in modern terms, he were watching a projection, not of moving pictures, but of diapositives. This primitive impression, however, is contradicted by those scenes in which the deceased is shown taking a personal part, like Sennedjem, in agricultural work, or hunting in a papyrus grove, like Menna. In such cases the representation is lifelike and the rigid schematization of the robot disappears. We are, in fact, given ample information as to the nature of the actual participation of the *Ka* in the life of the scenes depicted, in Chapter CX of 'The Book of the Dead', where the deceased declares, *inter alia*: 'That I may there be able to eat, drink, plough, take part in the harvest, fight, love . . .' in other words not only 'be present', but also 'participate'. Why, then, does the normal iconography relegate the *Ka* to the almost absent state of an automaton? The key to this interesting aesthetical problem, which has kindled the interest of numerous scholars and constitutes one of the typical manifestations of the Egyptian art of representation, may be found in the idea of reducing such figures to the simple value of *points d'appui*—in many cases the mere indication of the deceased's name suffices—in order that the volitive act of the *Ka* may reproduce the chosen theme and extract from it, at every moment, those sensations which a musician might experience when executing different pieces.

Outside the tombs the scenes generally have a documentary and narrative value glorifying the reigning sovereign. In the monumental ensemble they adorn the temple walls or the processional passages leading from the valley temples to the funerary temples. The realistic evocation is accentuated in scenes of highly dramatic content, a typical example being the Asiatics dying of starvation along the roads of Egypt—a testimony to the famine which was an actual fact during the reign of Unis (Fifth Dynasty), handed down to posterity on the limestone blocks of that king's 'sacred way' at Sakkâra (Plate 14).

The scene in question produces a direct impression on our sensibility, because the idealization—despite the realism—of the work projects it beyond the barriers of time into the immanence of eternity. It is a real 'archetype' of 'death by starvation', independent of time and place. The interlocking play of the emaciated limbs—almost like spider's legs—the deliberately angular rendering of the curves, accentuate

44

the pathos which the anatomical detail in itself is required to evoke. The arm of the dying parent in the central scene of the lower row, bent because it can no longer support the weight of the body, the almost exaggerated gesture of the woman at the beginning of the same row, devouring the parasites she has pulled out of her hair, and the raving figure attacking another wretch in the upper row—all these are details which make the scene a dramatic, vivid document with a descriptive functionality.

Of a similar realistic and naturalistic savour is the battle scene from the same 'sacred way' of Unis, but closer examination reveals at the same time the clever scenographic construction (Plate 15). The figures seem as if they were dancing, and the eurhythmic effect is heightened by the placing of the personages. The point of equilibrium is represented by the inter-section, carefully geometrical, of the legs of the two Egyptian warriors standing back to back in the centre of the scene. At the two extremities, two Asiatics are being slain: the one on the left, pierced by a dart, is turning a somersault with his legs in the air, while his colleague on the right is struck down by the dagger of the Egyptian who has attacked him. The whole scene is filled with movement, as if it were rotating around the central point of equilibrium. This bas-relief is also of great interest for the history of costume. Note the little knickers—real 'shorts'—worn by the warriors, which are even more prominent in the fragment from the latest excavations: an extremely rare testimony of a similar form of attire. In this fragment the point of equilibrium is similar to that in the preceding: the intersection in the centre of the warriors' legs.

It is in the early historic period that, together with scenes having a purely magical purpose, we can trace the origins of scenes possessing a narrative and descriptive character. On the slate palettes used for grinding malachite to make a cosmetic for the eyes, pictures are evolved, the intention of which is narrative. This is true of the hunting scenes as well as of the palette of Narmer commemorating the union of Upper and Lower Egypt under one crown. It is round the figure of the sovereign, the earthly incarnation of a divine principle and the apex of the State organization, that the narrative is centred. Unlike the representations of deceased commoners, the king's figure is almost always shown in action, striking down enemies or wild bulls, hunting beasts of prey, conferring with the gods or with his own subjects—never as a spectator, but always as an active agent. Here we have the fundamental difference between the scenes in private tombs and those glorifying the exploits of a sovereign. In the latter case, the intention is to link the name of the monarch with imperishable monuments, a fact which is also important from the religious point of view, since this was the actual reason why temples were constructed. In the instructions given by King Khety to his son Merikarēʿ, we read: 'Erect monuments to the gods; do this in order that the name of the builder may live again. . . .'

Names, according to Egyptian notions, had a definite value: they not only described things, but also shared in the 'essence' of the thing itself. In the

46

magical *grimoires*, whoever wished to harm a person had to have previous knowledge of the name which would be pronounced in the formulae of execration.

'Making one's name live', or in other words handing down the memory of oneself to posterity, operated on the same plane in the world to come, since it was believed that the phonetic vibrations of the person who read the name and formulae would have a vitalizing effect. We have already mentioned the funerary formulae inscribed on the walls of tombs and 'animated' by the voice of the priest who read them; they were all applications of that same principle which formed the basis of the laudatory autobiographical stelae begging the living to read them. 'It is certainly a useful thing,' states the scribe of the fourth Chester Beatty papyrus, 'if a name is in the mouths of the living.'

It was for this reason that in times of political and religious upheaval the names of an adversary and his followers were obliterated from tombs and temples. The monumental narrative dealt with various periods in the life of a sovereign, stressing the salient episodes. In the temple of Hatshepsut at Deir el-Bahri the scenes depict the birth of the queen, her travels, her coronation, the expedition to the land of Punt, etc. Apart from the Sinai graffiti showing King Sekhemkhet of the Third Dynasty in the act of slaying an enemy, the monumental complexes of Sahurē' and Unis show these Old Kingdom rulers taking part in military campaigns, just as at the beginning of the Middle Kingdom Montuhotep is shown waging war on the remains of the first temple at Deir el-Bahri and Ramesses II vanquishing the Libyans during the New Kingdom era. A guiding thread links the sovereigns of the first with those of the last dynasties, independent of the changing vicissitudes of the various periods: the affirmation of power pictorially proclaimed in the formal act of a Pharaoh slaying an enemy, in the long columns of fettered prisoners, in the snapshots of Pharaonic armies on the march towards fresh victories. This guiding thread ignores the obscure intermediate periods, the revolutions and foreign dominations, the memory of which was not preserved on imperishable monuments, designed only to record glorious events.

Side by side with the scenes of war are others showing the king paying homage to the gods, varying with the period and the religious centre. It is a friendly homage, a greeting of persons of equal rank, almost like that of a younger to an elder brother, and in any case there is none of the reverent aloofness that characterizes the relationship between the man in the street and a divinity. But the sovereign—and this is the important point—does not disdain to reap the ears of corn or to plough a furrow in the presence of the divine Nile, in the same attitude as a peasant. For here, more than in the exaltation of military glories, lies the real essence of Egypt, a country which to a greater degree than any other owed its civilization to agriculture. Just as the remote king of the early historical period is shown with a spade in his hand while he takes part in a religious ceremony, so, two thousand years later, does Ramesses III reap and plough at Medinet Habu. We can well understand the feeling of noble serenity that must have filled even the humblest *fellahin* of the period when they passed in front of the temple on which the highest authority in the land was shown performing the same actions as themselves.

From the technical point of view we may note that in the reliefs adorning the exteriors of temples, which were exposed to the weather, the figures were executed by hollowing out (*relief en creux*), while on the interior walls the figures were raised (*bas-relief*).

During the Old Kingdom there was a complete absence of any 'narrative' reference to the life of the owner of a tomb. The only exception was the episode of the funeral, and we are bound to ask ourselves why, side by side with representations of 'typical acts' based on a finalistic conception, room should have been found for these scenes connected with funerals. It must be borne in mind that all the scenes depicted in tombs were executed during the lifetime of the owner and are thus descriptions, not of something that had already taken place, but of something that had still to happen. And it was precisely in order that it might happen, in other words to bring about the events in conformity with a pre-arranged programme, that the representations of funerals were executed. For an ancient Egyptian, in fact, there was nothing more terrible than the danger of not receiving proper burial, of dying, for example, as a result of drowning in a river without the benefits of mummification and the rites ensuring immortality. Faced with such an eventuality, and with a view to avoiding it, he was at pains to entrust to the walls of his tomb an exact description of what he hoped would come to pass.

It is true that at Deshasheh and Sakkâra a few tombs contain scenes depicting sieges possessing a certain descriptive character, in which the long vertical ladders used by the besiegers even introduce new elements of perspective into the structure of the horizontal rows. But these are sporadic cases, real exceptions indicating the existence at the end of the Sixth Dynasty of new ideas on form. We are on the eve of a period of unrest and internal strife and it is interesting to note how the same siege motive with ladders recurs at the dawn of the Middle Kingdom on the already-mentioned temple of Montuhotep at Deir el-Bahri.

During the Middle Kingdom other currents became manifest and were superimposed on the crystallized schemes of the Old Kingdom. For example, in his tomb at el-Bersheh Djehutihotep takes a personal part in the hunting of birds and, though remaining seated on his stool in the typical attitude, he pulls the cord which closes the trap. This is a direct participation in the life of the composition. And for the first time, in the tomb of Antefoker, we see a private individual doing homage to the king whom he served during his lifetime. In the Old Kingdom period the sovereign had never been depicted in a private tomb, and, as H. Junker has observed, the fact can be related to the idea of 'impurity' connected with the tomb, from which the divine figure of the ruler had therefore to be excluded. The fact that, under the Middle Kingdom, this theme began to be treated and was subsequently developed during the New Kingdom era, shows that something new had happened, that the democratic revolution which suddenly broke out at the end of the Sixth Dynasty, and which we shall discuss later, had brought about changes—a more intimate relationship between the sovereign and his subjects which found its highest expression in the reigns of Amenophis III and IV. In the tomb of Kheruef at Thebes, the king is shown participating in the erection of the *djed* or pillar sacred to Osiris, a very important rite in the praxis of the cult. In the exercise of his functions the owner had taken part in this ceremony during his lifetime and he wished to perpetuate the memory of the event. We may note, incidentally, that the figure of Kheruef and his name were carefully chipped away by his adversaries after his death and that the tomb itself, a very beautiful one, was unfortunately given over to the flames. On the tomb of Khaemhet there is a reference to the *sed* jubilee in which Amenophis III took part, and at the same time the sovereign is shown distributing rewards to various officers. Haremhab is shown being acclaimed by his soldiers, the physician Nebamun in the act of administering medicine to a Syrian prince. And the various officials were fond of having themselves represented in the exercise of their functions, for instance Menna, the 'scribe of the fields', while measuring land. All these examples bear witness to the rise and development of new tendencies to which we shall return when we deal with the plastic arts.

CHAPTER FOUR

The plastic arts and royal iconography

'Royalty is a rank of splendour,' declared King Khety, and on the palette of Narmer the monarch's figure already emerges in the conventional way from among the other personages surrounding him. Another hierarchy existed among these latter, based on the same principle of proportional differences of stature. This was a simple and efficacious method, the origin of which can be traced back to the psychological processes of the ancient African rock-painters, who represented the 'king' and all beings of a supernatural character (frequently anthropomorphic-zoocephalic types) in larger dimensions than ordinary mortals. This convention was not limited to royal personages, for in historical times we find it used by private individuals in their tombs, where the deceased is generally represented—both in bas-reliefs and in statuary—in larger dimensions than his wife and children.

Graffiti on rocks and ivory plaques have preserved for posterity the images of early historical kings, as in the already-mentioned case of Sekhemkhet on Mount Sinai, or King Udimu taking part in the *sed* festival and, on another occasion, slaying a prisoner. Only one ivory statuette has transmitted the features of a sovereign, though an unknown one, from those still nebulous days when the monarchy was being consolidated after the union of Upper and Lower Egypt. In 1931 this statuette, now in the British Museum, was subjected to a thorough restoration, in the course of which it lost, at least to a certain extent, the accentuated character of an old man that had been hastily attributed to it by early scholars. On the other hand, there emerged the detail of the royal cape, the 'ermine' of those days, with its pattern of lozenges, the typical garb worn during the *sed* festival. The brow, seen in profile (Plate 16), follows the curve of the crown of Upper Egypt, and in the rhythm of the composition it balances the pronounced stoop of the shoulders. The arms are clearly visible beneath the cloak, from which only the hands emerge; these have now disappeared, but they must once have held the royal insignia. The charm of this figurine gives it more than a mere antiquarian value and is due to the fact that it bears witness to the achievement of a maturity in the rendering of expression. This unknown monarch of the first historical era seems already to contain all the 'religious' feeling for royalty that characterized royal iconography throughout the Old Kingdom period until the revolution at the end of the Sixth Dynasty, which resulted in a new attitude towards the sovereign, who in many respects was humanized. Here we are still in a period during which the sovereign was a god upon earth and had his own celestial paradise from which the rest of the populace was excluded. In the 'Pyramid Texts', the most ancient form of religious literature that has come down to us, we read of King Unis: 'Thou enterest into the gates of Heaven that are forbidden to the people.'

This exclusiveness, which meant that for the populace as a whole the after-life was confined to this world, must have been one of the causes, combined with other social and political factors, of the upheaval we have mentioned.

Obviously, royal iconography was bound to reflect the influence of such conceptions, which marked the abyss separating the figure of the monarch from the rest of the nation. This distinction was noticed by Capart, who, in his book entitled *Les débuts de l'art en Égypte*, wrote: 'For a long time afterwards, we can discern in monuments to private individuals the current opposed to official Pharaonic art. The same contrast which we have already noticed in reliefs, between official Pharaonic art and that of ordinary private individuals, is found in statuary, at all events during the first three dynasties.' The same author also notes the distinction, established by Schweinfurth in 1898, between '*Bauernkunst*' and '*Herrenkunst*'. For this reason we have preferred, in the present volume, to preserve this distinction, devoting one chapter to the so-called 'official' art and another to that executed for private individuals.

In addition to this, sculpture in the round and bas-reliefs are dealt with together in the chapters devoted to the plastic arts, notwithstanding the fact that, from the point of view of perspective, bas-reliefs are closely allied to painting. We have already mentioned, however, that for the Egyptians the bas-relief had the value of a statue projected on to a flat surface and in many cases took the place of statues. For this reason, the bas-relief was much closer to statuary than to painting in its rendering of the actual features of the personages represented and thus has considerable iconographical value. We shall not omit, however, to discuss the relationship between the bas-relief and painting in the chapter devoted to the latter. The sculptors, and in general all artists, were under the supervision of the High Priest of Ptah in Memphis, who bore the title of 'Supreme Master of the artists', and the influence exercised by the temple was thus direct.

The two statues of King Khasekhem of the Second Dynasty reveal a clear break with archaic ideas, especially as regards technique, since one of them was executed in slate. Wood and ivory could be carved with relative ease, but the same cannot be said of the hard basaltic rocks, such as diorite and porphyry, used in monumental Pharaonic art. When admiring the technical skill displayed in such works we cannot help feeling surprised when we examine the instruments used in their making. Bronze did not make its appearance until later, and the earliest instruments were made of copper, a ductile material which was liable to blunt without even scratching the rocks we have mentioned. The mystery surrounding the use of such instruments led J. de Morgan to formulate the theory that the Egyptians of those remote times knew of some method of 'tempering' copper which, by altering the molecular structure of the metal, made it harder than modern steel. The effect of such a process would not, however, have lasted for long, since the molecules would have resumed their original structure, and that explains why the instruments that have come down to us have the molecular structure of natural copper.

The technical skill achieved in the working of hard stones is proved not only by the slate plaque in the tomb of Hemaka, but also by the diorite vases of the early historical period, as well as by the clean cutting of the granite in the interior of the Great Pyramid, between the joints of which it is impossible to insert even the sharpest blade. Another ground for astonishment, besides the metal of which they are made, is the primitiveness of the instruments, which were cast in open moulds and then hammered. They comprise simple chisels of various sizes, sometimes sharpened at both ends, a rather broad and flat knife, a little axe for fashioning wood, and lastly saws of various sizes, drills and picks for detaching large blocks. The handles of these instruments were made of wood and their primitive aspect is in such strident contrast with the superb delicacy of the works produced that one is bound to suspect the existence of other technical means. And as a matter of fact a thousand years of experience with another technique made its contribution—that of polishing by means of abrasion, combined with physical strength and patience. This technique produced astonishing results. A vase of white and black syenite, found by Petrie at Hieraconpolis, is six inches high with a diameter of twenty-four inches, but as a result of careful abrasion the sides have been reduced to such thin sheets that the whole vase can be lifted with one finger!

By the time of the Third Dynasty, the acknowledged starting-point of the Old Kingdom, the art of sculpture had reached a definite stage of perfection, not only as regards technique, but also in its forms of expression. From this period, in fact, dates the statue of Zoser reproduced in Plate 4, the earliest life-size portrait of a king that has come down to us. It was found in the *serdab* of the step pyramid erected by this monarch and still retains vestiges of the colours which originally coated the limestone used: white for the mantle, brown for the skin, black for the hair and beard. The expression of the face is autocratic, without any trace of benevolence. The historical convention of dating the beginning of the Old Kingdom from this period finds support in its monumental splendour, its glory and creative genius, all of them elements characterizing the difference between architecture based on crude clay bricks and the use of lasting stone. This represents the transition from the ephemeral to the immortal, from the temporary to the permanent. As if it had been treated by a magical process, the organic material becomes 'petrified': the wooden beams of the ceilings, the half-open doors, the vegetable columns are all transformed into white limestone, though retaining intact their appearance and structure. The 'Pyramid Era' begins in the year 2700 B.C., when Memphis was the capital of the kingdom.

If, despite the ravages of time and the vandalism of men, the great monumental complexes and the statues still bear witness to the stage of 'petrifaction' and the progress of art, it is only the carved bas-reliefs in the deep recesses of the tombs that have managed to survive and have preserved for us the youthful image of Zoser taking part in the 'race' during the ceremony of the *sed* (Plate 9). This was a kind of jubilee celebrated several times during the life of a ruler, a periodical 'bath of youth', but it was also a clear demonstration, in the presence of the forty-two representatives of the administrative departments into which Egypt was divided, that the king's powers were unimpaired and that he was still capable of fulfilling his function.

Under the following dynasty, the Fourth, the mania for building in stone became intense and inspired the construction of the great pyramids. The first sovereign of this period, Snefru, appears in a valuable fragment of a bas-relief discovered during the excavation of the pyramid at Dahshûr, which clearly shows the application of the geometrical canon (Plate 17). The king is represented while receiving the breath of life from a divinity with a feline head, and the point of equilibrium of the composition is provided by the contact of the noses. Notwithstanding the fragmentary character of this work, what is left is enough to show the definite stage that had also been reached in the technique of bas-relief.

Also from the Fourth Dynasty are the portraits of the builders of the three most important pyramids, Khufu, Khafrē' and Menkaurē', better known by the Greek versions of their names: Cheops, Chephren and Mycerinus.

By the irony of fate, the only image that has come down to us of the builder of the greatest monument of Antiquity is a tiny ivory statuette found by Petrie among the ruins of the temple of Abydos (Plate 18).

The sovereign is shown seated on his throne with the *flagellum*, or flail, in his right hand, while his left rests on the upper portion of his leg. The face is rather broad, with the brow enframed by the crown; the lines of the mouth and the somewhat square chin give the personage a markedly wilful expression. Nor can we deny that there is a certain 'monumental' character in this work, despite its small dimensions.

Wilful, too, is the expression of Chephren in the diorite statue now in the museum at Cairo, with his broad face and prominent cheekbones (Plate 19). The false beard is fused with the chin, of which it becomes a prolongation giving balance to the broadness of the face. The artist's endeavour to achieve representation of the 'divine upon earth' is obvious. The device of not showing the pupils, as if the eyeballs were turned in upon themselves, heightens the effect of introspection characteristic of other funerary statues. It is a contemplation of other spheres of existence, a detachment from surrounding reality, but this does not imply 'absence'. On the contrary, Egyptian statues never give the impression of an organism in repose that could be correlated with the idea of 'relaxing', but reveal a concentration of strength, a dynamism, which, though it may be only in a potential state, is none the less expressed and perceptible.

The visage of Chephren is enframed by the *nemes*, the typical cloth headgear descending on either side at the front in horizontal pleats, while the *uraeus* or sacred serpent lies on the forehead. Modern scholars agree in identifying the features of the enigmatic

Sphinx, near the second pyramid at Gizeh, as being those of this monarch.

Of Mycerinus we possess a number of statues, which, however, have no definite value from the point of view of evolutionary analysis. Interesting, nevertheless, is the group now in Boston (Mass.), in which the sovereign is shown with his wife, who embraces his waist with her arm in token of affection. The queen is here represented in the same dimensions as her consort, a fact which denotes the esteem in which she was held. To the same school of sculpture belongs the series of 'mythologico-geographical' works discovered by Reisner in the temple vestibule of the third pyramid. Here the sovereign appears in the company of a goddess and a personification of a *nome*, or administrative district of Egypt. As there were forty-two of these, we may assume that an equal number of groups of statuary originally existed. In one of them the king is in the centre between the goddess Hathor and the personification of the *nome* of Aphroditopolis. The figure of the sovereign, wearing the crown of Upper Egypt, is slightly taller than those of the two ladies, and he stands a pace in front of them, though he holds both his arms parallel to the axis of his body—an attitude identical with that seen in the Boston group.

The Fourth and Fifth Dynasties are rightly considered to have been the 'golden age' of Egyptian art. The zenith achieved by sculpture at this time is clearly proved by the stupendous 'royal head', still comparatively little known because of the recent date (April 1957) of its discovery at Abusir by the Swiss-

German archaeological mission (Plates 20, 21).
The head is life-size, executed in greenish grey slate
from the Wadi Hammâmât. The features are those
of a man in the prime of life and the delicately treated
curves have a plastic softness which is exceptional
if we consider the nature of the material used. The
important point is that the material is obliterated in
the interests of form and expression. The nose is
delicate and at the same time robust, the orbital cavity
moulds the finely delineated eye, which is artificially
prolonged towards the temple. The crown, the
upper part of which has unfortunately been broken,
has bold and dynamic lines. Though the personage
the artist intended to represent has not yet been
identified, the name of Userkaf, the first monarch of
the Fifth Dynasty, has been suggested, a gigantic
head of whom, in granite and admirably fashioned,
is preserved in the Cairo Museum.

The rhythmical grace of the bas-reliefs dating
from this period is revealed in the lithe forms of the
women bearing offerings in the temple of Sahurē‘,
the longitudinal style of which was later copied
on the walls of the tomb of Ptahhotep. We have
already mentioned the bas-reliefs on the walls of the
'sacred way' of King Unis, the last sovereign of the
Fifth Dynasty, and we have also analysed some of
their aesthetical aspects. The walls of the pyramids,
or rather the apartments within them, were decorated
at this time with the religious and magical texts to
which we have several times referred—the 'Pyramid
Texts'.

To the Sixth Dynasty belongs the copper statue of

Pepy I, a work unique in its kind. It was found in fragments by Quibell among the ruins of the temple at Hieraconpolis and after being reassembled was found to be 5 feet 7 inches high. Originally it was conceived as a wooden statue covered by copper plates, which are now all that remains of it. Traces of gilding lead one to suppose that the statue must have originally been completely enclosed in a covering of gold, and this is confirmed, at all events theoretically, by a decree of Pepy II, in which mention is made of a statue in 'Asian bronze, covered with gold'. Though the crown, presumably of precious metal, has disappeared, the face retains an expression which is both dignified and serene. Two other statuettes, now at Brooklyn, show the same sovereign in two different attitudes. In one of them, carved out of green slate, he is shown in the act of worshipping, with two round bowls in his hands—the only occasion on which this attitude is found during the Old Kingdom period, though it afterwards became general under the New Kingdom. In the other, which is of alabaster, the king is wearing the *sed* mantle and the crown of Upper Egypt, while the sceptre and flail are crossed upon his breast and a falcon sits on the upper portion of the throne. In this latter statuette the king's pose is reminiscent of that of Osiris, the patron of the dead, though it differs in that the head-dress has no plumes, while the royal mantle replaces the wrappings of the mummy. The comparison is, however, interesting, and despite the presence of the solar principle represented by the falcon, the influence of the religion of Osiris, i.e. of the poor, is evident.

We have now reached the eve of the end of the Old Kingdom, which had lasted for five centuries and of which the pyramid is perhaps the most expressive symbol: at the summit, unapproachable and intangible, was the king-god, who presided over the hierarchy of functionaries down to the foundations symbolizing the great mass of common people. And while the summit, soaring upwards to the sky, proclaimed a stellar and solar doctrine reserved for its own exclusive use, the people turned towards the figure of Osiris, whose human characteristics of a deified sovereign were more readily understood than abstract theologies. The contrast between the solar doctrine and that of Osiris left its traces in the 'Pyramid Texts', where we even find anathemas directed against Osiris: 'Do not allow Osiris to come here, for his coming would be an evil thing.'

The hereditary nature of titles and noble offices, which for a long time remained *ad personam*, brought about a decentralization which it soon became impossible to stop and which split Egypt up into a number of principalities with a tendency to become as far as possible autonomous and independent of the crown. Contemporary with these disruptive forces in the State organism was a strong migratory movement from the north-east of Mesopotamia, which progressively affected the districts of Amurru, Canaan and Palestine. The struggle for power among the individual *nomarchs*, the presence of mercenary and foreign troops in the interior of the country, together with the gradual but continual infiltration of uncontrollable elements across the too far-flung frontiers, and in addition the ill-feeling caused among the populace by the application of the 'class system' in funeral rites with regard to the 'celestial' paradise, were the principal factors that gave birth to the social upheaval which occurred during the reign of Pepy II. This monarch, who ascended the throne at the age of six on the death of his brother Merenrē', had the longest reign in history—no less than ninety-four years on end! The papyrus of a later period which narrates these events assumes a dramatic tone: 'Gates, columns and walls burned with the houses' and 'gold, lapis lazuli, silver and turquoise hung from the necks of slaves, while ladies walked through the streets in rags'. Nobody worried any more about tilling the soil and famine spread throughout the land: 'Everywhere the wheat is dead and the cattle weep for the state of the country: men live on herbs and drink water.'

But one of the aims had been achieved: '. . . The poor man has achieved the state of the Ennead' (i.e. the right to become 'divine', which previously the Pharaoh alone had held).

The curtain fell on the scene of a kingdom in dissolution, and darkness descended upon Egypt for two centuries. The Middle Kingdom arose thanks to the princes of the new capital, Thebes, but the background had undergone a profound change. Even though the idea of royal divinity contrived to survive, its psychological point of gravity had shifted, and a policy of compromise was established between the powerful, autonomous feudal caste which was beginning to usurp titles, insignia and functions that

PLATE 19. Detail of statue of King Chephren. Diorite. From Gizeh. Fourth Dynasty. Height of original 66 inches; 168 cm. *Cairo, Museum.*

PLATE 20. Head of a sovereign. Slate. From the excavations at Abusir.
Original lifesize. *Cairo, Museum.*

Plate 21. Cf. Plate 20.

PLATE 22. Wooden statuette of King Sesostris I. From el Lisht. Twelfth Dynasty. Height 22½ inches; 57 cm. *Cairo, Museum.*

PLATE 23. Anthropocephalic Sphinx with the features of King Sesostris III.
Diorite. Original 16¾ × 29 inches; 42.5 × 73.5 cm.
New York, Metropolitan Museum.

PLATE 24. Detail from the painted limestone sarcophagus of Queen Kawit. From Deir el-Bahri. Eleventh Dynasty. *Cairo, Museum.*

PLATE 25. Small ivory Sphinx, grasping an Egyptian in its claws. Hyksos Period. Length 2⅜ inches; 6 cm. *London, British Museum.*

PLATE 26. Bearers of offerings. Polychrome bas-relief in the temple of Queen
Hatshepsut at Deir el-Bahri. Eighteenth Dynasty.

PLATE 27. Detail of the slate statue of King Tuthmosis III. From Karnak. Height of the whole statue 79 inches; 200 cm. Eighteenth Dynasty. *Cairo, Museum.*

PLATE 28. Amenophis III. Bas-relief in the tomb of Kheruef at Thebes.
Eighteenth Dynasty.

PLATE 29. Basalt statue attributed to Ramesses III. Nineteenth Dynasty. Height 76¼ inches; 194 cm. *Turin, Museum.*

PLATE 30. Sethos I with the statuette of the goddess Māʻet. Bas-relief from the temple at Abydos. Nineteenth Dynasty.

PLATE 31. Fragment of a statue representing a princess of the family of Ramesses II. Nineteenth Dynasty. Height of original 28¾ inches; 73 cm. *Cairo, Museum.*

PLATE 32. Ramesses III hunting. Temple of Medinet Habu. Nineteenth Dynasty.

PLATE 33. The "Divine Worshipper" of Amun, Amenardis I, on the knees of the god. Headless group in green faience. From Karnak. Twenty-fifth Dynasty. Height of the original, 13·5 cm. *Cairo, Museum.*

PLATE 34. The goddess Hathor in the shape of a cow protecting the noble Psamtik. Saitic period. Length of original 41¼ inches; 105 cm. *Cairo, Museum.*

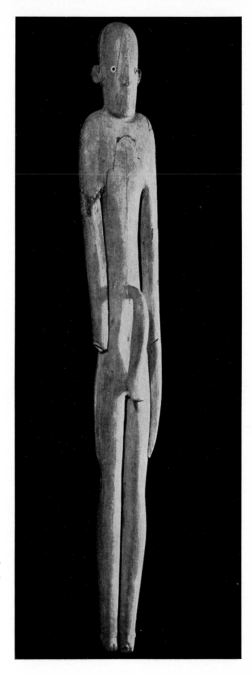

PLATE 35. Prehistoric human figure in ivory. Negadah Period.
Cairo, Museum.

PLATE 36. Negadah dancer. Terracotta. *Bremen, Museum.*

PLATE 37. Wooden statue of Kaaper, the "Village Sheikh". From Sakkâra. End of Fourth – beginning of Fifth Dynasty. Height of original $43\frac{1}{4}$ inches; 110 cm. *Cairo, Museum.*

PLATE 38. Painted limestone statue of the High Priest Ranofer, from his tomb at Sakkâra. Fifth Dynasty. Height 71 inches; 180 cm. *Cairo, Museum.*

PLATE 39. Painted limestone statue of a scribe. Fifth Dynasty.
Height 20 inches; 51 cm. *Cairo, Museum.*

PLATE 40. Detail of a stuccoed wooden statue with inlaid eyes. From Sakkâra. Fifth Dynasty. Only the head and shoulders exist. Height 27¼ inches; 69 cm. *Cairo, Museum.*

PLATE 41. Painted limestone group showing Akhi and his family. From Sakkâra.
End of Fifth Dynasty. *Cairo, Museum.*

PLATE 42. Detail of the polychrome statues in the hypogeum of Irukaptah at Sakkâra. In the upper row, slaughtering of animals.

PLATE 43. The nobleman Ti hunting in a papyrus thicket. Mural bas-relief in his tomb at Sakkâra. Fifth Dynasty.

PLATE 44. "The Vintage". Bas-relief in the tomb of Nefer-her-Ptah at Sakkâra. Fifth Dynasty.

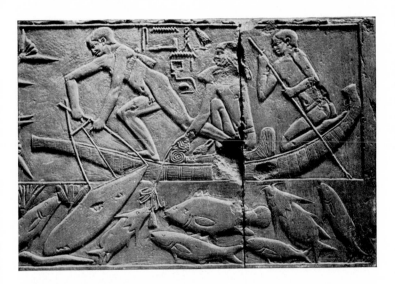

PLATE 45. Fishing scene. Bas-relief in the tomb of Kagemni at Sakkâra.
Sixth Dynasty.

PLATE 46. The lame herdsman in the tomb of Ptahhotpe at Sakkâra. Sixth Dynasty.

PLATE 47. The slave-girl Ishat grinding corn. Painted limestone. From Sakkâra.
Fifth Dynasty. 14 inches; 35.5 cm. *Cairo, Museum.*

PLATE 48. Woman carrying offerings. Statuette in painted wood from the tomb of Meketrēʻ at Deir el-Bahri. Eleventh Dynasty. Height about 27½ inches; 70 cm. *Cairo, Museum.*

PLATE 49. Head of a woman, in wood. From el-Lisht. Twelfth Dynasty.
Height of original 3⅜ inches; 8.5 cm. *Cairo, Museum.*

PLATE 50. Limestone group showing Thai and his wife Naia. From Sakkâra. Nineteenth Dynasty. Height 35½ inches; 90 cm. *Cairo, Museum.*

PLATE 51. Detail from a bas-relief in the tomb of the Vizier Ramose in Thebes.
Eighteenth Dynasty.

had previously been the exclusive perquisites of the Pharaohs. They even reached the point of using the same official language employed by the king in his decrees, and artists gave the royal features to statues of private individuals.

Of this first phase, still under the influence of the preceding upheaval, a striking testimony is provided by the statue of Montuhotep now in the museum at Cairo, which is coarsely executed and almost brutal in its chromatic aggressiveness; it lacks all finish and is almost tragic in its static immobility. The massive, lifeless legs form parallels to the cubic throne, while the very thick neck fails to provide an adequate transition from the trunk to the head, which is surmounted by the red crown of Lower Egypt. The eyes seem to be staring into the void and the expression of the face resembles that of a condemned man rather than that of a ruling sovereign. In the Metropolitan Museum at New York there is a similar statue, differing only in that the subject is shown standing instead of seated. It is true that later on the Middle Kingdom knew periods of splendour and glory, but faith in general had been shaken and scepticism was beginning to spread. This was the period during which mundane pleasures were exalted at banquets: 'Do what thou wilt on this earth until the day of thy death, for death will not heed thy lamentations and tears will not liberate any man from the other world. Spend therefore thy days in rejoicing! It is certain that none can take his riches with him! It is certain that not one of those who set out for the other world will ever return!'

When Amenemhet I, in the twentieth year of his reign, appointed his son Sesostris I co-regent, he admonished him in these terms: 'Beware of thy subordinates, do not approach them and do not remain alone. Trust not thy brother, know no friends and have no intimates, for they will avail thee nothing. When thou sleepest, watch over thyself, since in the days of adversity we have no allies. . . .' These are the words of a father conscious of the weighty inheritance he is bequeathing to his heir, but they are certainly not the language of a 'god'.

In their search for equilibrium the artists of the Twelfth Dynasty wavered between the 'human' model of a king and his traditional 'type'. In the museum at Cairo there is a wooden statue of Sesostris wearing the crown of Upper Egypt (Plate 22), and a counterpart to this, wearing the red crown, is in New York. The rule of the walking pose is carefully respected: the left leg is thrust forward, the left arm raised and bent as it holds the crook, while the right arm hangs parallel to the axis of the body, with the sceptre (now missing) clasped in the hand. Nevertheless, despite the canonical model, the artist has to some extent 'humanized' the face: the more vivacious eyes seem to avoid the introspective characteristic of the Old Kingdom and to concentrate on observing the world around them. In other words we have here a living being rather than one absorbed in the contemplation of higher planes of existence. This impression is confirmed by the stone statue of the same sovereign found at el-Lisht. The body is rigidly conventional; since he did not know how to interpret the new trends, the artist took refuge in strict classicism, and yet the face—although the body is a mere automaton —has a life of its own, with a mildly benevolent smile which was accentuated during the following periods, until it became almost stereotyped under the New Kingdom.

Two fundamental tendencies are perceptible in the statuary of the Middle Kingdom. The first, which developed in the north, had as its salient characteristic the search for the 'human' motive and to it belong the works we have mentioned above. The second, which developed in the south, was of a completely different character, since it laid stress on a realism carried to extremes and on autocratic features going back to Old Kingdom models. Note, for example, the mask of Sesostris III on the body of a sphinx (Plate 23). The protruding underlip and chin, the accentuated cheekbones, the drooping corners of the mouth and the general expression of the face remind us of the features of the statue of King Zoser. In this particular case the combination with the body of a sphinx makes the notion of humanization even more remote, and this is also true of the sphinx with the face of Amenemhet III. Pharaonic iconography evolved in accordance with these two tendencies: some accepted the warning of the revolution and adapted themselves to the new conception of the sovereign's personality; others rebelled against it with all their strength and for this reason wished to be associated with mythical animals in order to stress their aloofness from mankind, just as Chephren had done in the days of the Old Kingdom. But the analogy was purely external, since the changes that had taken place had radically modified the substantial structure. The sphinx of Chephren and the haughty expression of Zoser were based on foundations that had now been demolished for ever. The drooping corners of the mouth in the countenance of Sesostris III and the expression on the face of Amenemhet III in the statue from Hawara and in that now in Cambridge do not denote a gap between the divine and the human, but are an expression of mundane preoccupations.

The bas-reliefs introduce a few new notions, such as the weeping cow we have already mentioned, and at the same time they reveal a reaction against the period of the social upheaval. On the same sarcophagus of Queen Kawit showing the scene of the weeping cow we find the theme of the maidservants waiting upon the queen: fresh milk is brought to her in a bowl delicately held with two fingers, while a maid is carefully arranging the coiffure of the noble lady, whose neck is adorned with a triple necklace of jewels and her wrist with a heavy bracelet. Only a short time before 'gold and lapis lazuli were hanging from the necks of slave-girls . . .' The anti-revolutionary bias is obvious and is stressed by the total lack of ornaments on the body of the maid (Plate 24). Nor is this an isolated case. On the sarcophagus of Queen Ashayet, also of the Eleventh Dynasty, we see the lady comfortably seated while she enjoys the perfume of a flower. Behind her, a maid is waving a fan above a jar of perfume, so as to spread the smell, and her only ornament is a pair of rings on her ankles.

To the Middle Kingdom also belong a number of statues of the cubic type which were later given further development. We have already mentioned the theory of the derivation of this form from a stage in sculptural experience.

The invasion of the Semitic Hyksos during the Fifteenth and Sixteenth Dynasties paralysed all artistic activity. The occupying forces made no personal contribution, but in the course of their attempts to suppress every form of nationalism in the country they had conquered, they eventually assumed its customs and usages. The names of some of their rulers—Khian, Jacob, Apopi, etc.—have been perpetuated on scarabs, which were used, not as amulets or ornaments, but as seals by the tax-collectors.

A little ivory sphinx from this period, of the anthropocephalic type, now in the British Museum, is shown in the act of tearing an Egyptian to pieces with its claws. This is one of the few specimens of Hyksos art that have come down to us (Plate 25).

In addition to an oppressive regime and certain unpleasant diseases, the Hyksos introduced into Egypt the horse, and with it more rapid means of communication, both in peace and in war. The first mention of chariots is found on the Carnarvon plaque, and obviously refers to those of the Hyksos in flight during the Egyptian revolt.

This revolt was brought about by the Theban kings and marks the end of the Middle and the beginning of the New Kingdom. It occurred in 1580 B.C. and Amosis was the first sovereign of the Eighteenth Dynasty. Representations of the horse are widespread in New Kingdom bas-reliefs and paintings, and also in models (Plate C).

By way of reaction against the period of oppression, Egyptian policy now turned towards the expansion of the frontiers and military glory. Under Tuthmosis I the Egyptian armies advanced beyond the Third Cataract in Nubia and reached the banks of the Euphrates in Syria. These conquests, however, were not consolidated and Tuthmosis II had to deal with several risings. He was an illegitimate son, whose irregular position as regards succession to the throne had to be remedied by means of his marriage to his step-sister Hatshepsut, a legitimate daughter of his father. After the death of her husband, Hatshepsut assumed the guardianship of her stepson, the future Tuthmosis III, who was still a minor, and she became co-regent. But supported by the priests of Amun and fired by unbridled ambition, she soon succeeded in depriving her ward of his royal functions and became sole and undisputed sovereign.

Disdaining military expeditions, she preferred to devote herself to commercial enterprises, which brought her from distant lands spices, perfumes, precious woods and ivory, gold and exotic animals. The memory of these exploits has been immortalized on the walls of the magnificent temple built for her at Deir el-Bahri by her architect and favourite Senmut. Since she found it necessary to legalize, at least to some extent, her usurpation of the royal functions, Hatshepsut proclaimed that she was of divine origin, and on the walls of her temple she caused bas-reliefs to be made showing the various phases of her origin:

the god visiting the queen mother, the preparations made by the gods to celebrate the happy event, down to the actual birth. Together with these are scenes showing her baptism with the Water of Life by two divinities, her travels and her coronation as Queen of Upper and Lower Egypt. The style of these reliefs is derived from Old Kingdom models and constitutes a kind of neo-classicism. The bearers of offerings have the same dimensions as the antique models and the faces remind us of the carvings of Snefru's time (Plate 26).

Fully aware of the singularity of a matriarchate in Egyptian dynastic history, Hatshepsut assumed typically masculine costumes and poses, including even the wearing of a false beard, also perpetuated in the iconography of the anthropocephalic sphinx. Even the outlines of her breasts are flattened, both in statues and in bas-reliefs, among these being that on the obelisk she erected at Karnak, in which she appears before her 'divine father' Amun wearing the *khepresh* or blue crown, the use of which by Egyptian rulers began under this dynasty.

After the death of Hatshepsut, Tuthmosis III re-ascended the throne and indulged in a systematic destruction of everything that might have perpetuated the memory of his aunt and guardian. For this reason the Deir el-Bahri reliefs have come down to us in a sadly mutilated state; nearly everywhere the name of the queen has been carefully chipped away and replaced by that of the new sovereign.

The latter, returning to the tradition of military campaigns established by his grandfather Tuthmosis I, regained control of Syria and Palestine, and, after seizing one of the Phoenician seaports and occupying Kadesh, the citadel of his enemies, crossed the Euphrates and defeated the Mitannites. In seventeen successful campaigns, he expanded the frontiers of the kingdom to an extent never known before and made himself feared and respected by the neighbouring Assyrians and Babylonians, who hastened to send him tributes and offers of friendship.

Royal statuary now entered upon a period of decline which, if we exclude the Amarna interlude, achieved its climax of expression in the statue of Ramesses II now in the museum at Turin (Plate 29). This decline is characterized by a diminution of dramatic feeling and a relaxation of the dynamic tension. The countenance is idealized until it becomes a stereotyped smile (Plate 27), while the oriental luxury, together with the fashion of wearing light materials with a thousand folds, led to a Baroque tendency in which the artists of the period willingly sought refuge.

The aesthetic canon prescribed elongated models, but the elaboration of formal elegance suffocated the immediacy of expression: the figures are cleverly fashioned shells, but empty. Only in the reign of Amenophis III, the father of the schismatic Akhenaten, do we find a certain spiritualization and original ideas, as in the colossal quartzite head now in the British Museum. In the already-mentioned tomb of Kheruef the king appears both as a participant in the ceremony of the erection of the *djed* and seated on his throne (Plate 28). This figure merits special study, since it throws an imaginary bridge across the revolution of Akhenaten and provides a link with the following Dynasty, the Nineteenth, to which belongs the statue of Ramesses II in Turin. The latter work ignores completely the revolutionary influence of Amarna: the body is modelled on canonical New Kingdom lines and should be compared with the figure of Amenophis III. Identical are the head-dress, the blue crown, as also worn by Hatshepsut, the attitude of the body with one arm raised at an angle while the hand grasps the *heka* sceptre and the other arm more or less reposing in the plane. Identical is the position of the legs, while the feet are enclosed in the same type of sandals. The difference, in the statue of Ramesses, lies in the greater care devoted to the folds of the draperies, a sign—as we have already said—of evident decadence, and in the relaxation of the inner dynamic tension, still found in the bas-relief of Amenophis. Here we have, in the midst of the revolutionary era, a revival of old formulae which were no longer 'felt', and to these must be added the defects of the age. The pleasing elegance of the attire makes it possible for the artist to avoid all sculptural effort by concentrating on the details; the gentleness of the features, already noticeable in Tuthmosis III, here becomes weakness, accentuated by the lowered glance, while the hieratical attitude saves the work from those legacies of Amarna still to be seen in the relaxed attitude of Tutankhamun as represented on the back of his throne and in other carvings (Plate 84). A good example of carving in plastered and painted wood is the youthful bust from the tomb of Tutankhamun

73

(Plate D). The identification is still doubtful and some scholars, judging by the type of crown, think that it represents Queen Ankhesenamun, the sovereign's wife.

In the statue of Ramesses, the Amarna trend towards the grotesque, the nudist realism of bodily deformity, the violation of the traditional canon in its most intimate essence, are carried to the opposite extreme, resulting in a harmony of forms, with the body half concealed by the folds of the robe, and a complete revival of the traditional canon. If the reign of Tutankhamun can be considered as a kind of 'no man's land' in which the posthumous effects of Akhenaten's revolution were sifted and absorbed, the Nineteenth Dynasty shows that the digestion of these elements was complete; even the dregs did not manage to survive. Bas-reliefs, too, inevitably reflected the symptoms of the times, and Sethos I in the act of making an offering in the temple at Abydos is a significant example (Plate 30). The refinement of execution and formal elegance are undeniable, but something of the grandeur of Pharaonic art is missing. That potential 'force', which was so vivid in Old Kingdom statues, is here replaced by an intimate languor, reminiscent of a beautiful Baroque clock the spring of which has been broken. The artist, as we have said, concentrates on the details, and thus we have sculptural descriptions of elaborate wigs with varying superstructures. The princess of the household of Ramesses II (his wife or daughter) is wearing such a head-dress surmounted by a crown of *uraei*, like those of the goddess Isis (Plate 31). The face,

74

despite the missing nose, has a charm of its own which is continued in the delicate form of the arm, while the glance is lowered as in the statue of Ramesses II.

The New Kingdom was the period during which the horse dominated temple reliefs, being shown while charging the enemy or drawing the Pharaoh to victory in his war chariot. The adversaries form a compact mass of bodies in wildly disordered poses and above them hovers the plumed charger with its forefeet raised. Sethos I is represented in this way while fighting at Kadesh or against the Libyans, or in the act of overthrowing the fortresses of the Canaanites or during the attack on Yenoam. The motive of the chariot wheel introduces a new element into the composition, especially in the scene of the defeat of the Hittites, in which the fleeing enemies are themselves using chariots, the diminishing proportions giving an effect of perspective to the scene which is normally quite absent from bas-reliefs.

These large mural compositions reflect the 'thirst for glory' of this imperialistic period: the urge to entrust to stone the imperishable memory of one's own glory, the massacres (from which the Egyptian soldiers are invariably excluded, not one of them being even pierced by a dart) and finally the inevitable victory. These paeans resound from one wall to another, on the swift wings of the battle-horses, interspersed with scenes depicting the hunting of wild animals—as in the Ramesses III reliefs at Medinet Habu. Here the living tension of the scene, the climax of which is centred upon the speed of the horses, is broken—giving a fine effect of suspended drama—by the immobility of the wild bulls lying dead amidst the undergrowth, while the oblique line of the pond gives the scene a sense of dimensional depth which it would otherwise lack. The escorting troops in the lower row are an elegant border: note the play of their intersecting legs and the slight raising of the feet, while the system of perspective employed gives a clear view of the soldiers in the various ranks (Plate 32).

But the temple reliefs of this period, crystallizing as they do the last shouts of victory, were the swansong of Pharaonic art. The parabola which had begun two thousand years before was showing signs of senility. Even if individual gleams of light still shone in the midst of the inexorable decay, they were ends in themselves—will-o'-the-wisps in the cemetery of the Pharaohs.

During the Twentieth Dynasty the state of internal dissolution is abundantly proved by the judicial reports of proceedings against criminals, who formed organized bands and systematically plundered the royal necropolis at Thebes. The originals of these reports have come down to us in various papyri, among them those discovered by Abbott and Amherst, and their systematic collection and publication is due to T. E. Peet. From them the connivance of the public authorities with the criminals becomes clear and this was undoubtedly the gravest symptom of administrative decadence. In his verbatim statement, Amenpenefer, a bandit chief, declares among other things: 'I took twenty gold *deben* which were my share [of the loot] and gave them to the district scribe, Khaemapet, who set me free.'

The Twenty-first Dynasty saw the reign of the priests of Amun, and Pinedjem I seems to have dedicated part of his time to the restoration of the despoiled royal mummies, among them those of Tuthmosis I, Amenophis I, Sethos I, Ramesses II and Ramesses III, and to have tried to prevent, as far as possible, the activities of the thieves. It was a vain effort, for his successor had to continue the work of restoration on other royal mummies. There is some justification for assuming that the Twenty-first Dynasty coincided with the so-called 'low era' which began in 1085 B.C.

The kingdom gradually disintegrated; the impossibility of exercising control over the outlying regions brought about a reawakening of the subject peoples, until, during the Twenty-fifth Dynasty (712–663 B.C.), Egypt was conquered by the Ethiopians and governed from Napata in the Sudan, while at Thebes authority was in the hands of the 'Divine Worshipper of Amun', a female priestly function showing clear traces of the influence of the local divinity. A kind of Renaissance, one of those 'will-o'-the-wisps' we have already mentioned, can be detected in the arts and became stronger under the following dynasty; it relaxed to a certain extent the inhibitions of classical form and somewhat unusual poses began to appear in official statues, e.g. the very human embrace of Amun and his 'Divine Worshipper' Amenardis, shown seated on the knees of the god who clasps her in his arms (Plate 33). The importance of

77

this work is not due to the pose alone, for much cruder and more daring poses are found in small private statues and amulets, but to the fact that such plastic forms were accepted by so-called official art.

With the Twenty-sixth Dynasty begins the last period of Egyptian national history and the last flicker of the artistic flame. The two capitals, Sais and Memphis, gave their names to the trends prevailing at this time: Saitic and neo-Memphitic art. There was a return to the archaic denoting an intimate need to draw no longer existing strength from the original models, which were copied without any attempt to attenuate old age or ugliness (Plate 6 and Plate E). The stone, basalt or serpentine, was polished until it resembled the smooth surface of a mirror, while stylization was carried to extremes. Cold and un-communicative, the works were technically well executed, their details were carefully finished, gone over and polished, but they are infinitely remote (Plate 34). The bas-reliefs, though they imitate the Old Kingdom style, exaggerate the process of over-refinement, the earliest examples of which date from the Ramesside period of the New Kingdom.

After the Twenty-sixth Dynasty Egypt was con-quered by Cambyses, and after the Thirtieth by Alexander the Great. The works of art produced at this period were mechanical copies of what already existed, on which were superimposed the new trends introduced by the conquerors. This resulted in hybrid models of the syncretism which preceded the gnostic era, during which an attempt was made to amalgamate and fuse the most widely divergent religious tendencies, even to the point of associating the symbols of the newborn Christian faith with those of the Pharaonic religion. This period, completely apart from the original thread, is—for that very reason—outside the scope of the present study.

CHAPTER FIVE

The plastic arts and private iconography

THE fact that in the preceding pages we have
given a concise account of ancient Egyptian history
—even though it was limited to the background of
Pharaonic art—may simplify the task of dealing with
the plastic arts as applied to private iconography.
We must, however, make it clear at once that their
line of development did not always run parallel with
that of 'official' art, or in other words royal iconography, but from time to time either came closer to
it or departed from it, in accordance with trends
obviously influenced by social and political factors.

The 'corpus' of images of private individuals during
the historical period is provided by the representations
on tombs in the form either of bas-reliefs or of statues.
To show the difference between this phase and the
pre-dynastic period, we reproduce two figures
(Plates 35, 36), one a male figure in ivory, and the
other, in terracotta, representing a female dancer.
Both of these date from the Negadah period, which
preceded the historical period by some thousands of
years. The linear immobility of the ivory statuette has
its counterpart in the dynamism of this prehistoric
ballerina: nevertheless, we are still a long way from
the times when the 'canon' will begin to enclose
the limbs of statues in its rigid and mathematical
grip.

The first images of deceased persons make their appearance during the First Dynasty, the period to which are assigned the stelae found by Zaki Saad at Helwan. The deceased is represented seated before the table of offerings—a canonical attitude which will retain its validity throughout all subsequent periods. The statues are somewhat crude, but they too have poses and attitudes which will be repeated during the following centuries. A figure of a woman, on somewhat cubic lines, is now in the museum at Naples; in it the left arm, lying diagonally across the lap, reminds us of the pose of the statuette of King Khasekhem.

To the Third Dynasty belong the already-mentioned wooden panels of Hesirē', placed in the niches instead of the corresponding statues.

Nevertheless, at the beginning of the Old Kingdom, the bas-relief was already in line with the great architecture and the sculptural conceptions that distinguish the period.

To the beginning of the Fourth Dynasty, and more precisely to the reign of Snefru, belongs the painted limestone group of Rahotep and his wife Nefret, reproduced in almost every book dealing with Egyptian art. These are 'effective' pieces, especially as regards the perfect preservation of the chromatic values and the synthetic fusion of the forms beneath the white tunic of Nefret, but the total lack of expression in the faces, so remote from the powerful masks of a Zoser, reduces them to the level of competent bourgeois statuary. Far more important is the likewise well-known statue of Ka-aper (Plate 37), which Mariette's workmen nicknamed 'the village sheikh', on account of its striking resemblance to the sheikh of their own village. This work can be dated from the end of the Fourth or the beginning of the Fifth Dynasty, and although it retains the canonical attitude of standing figures, the personality of Ka-aper emerges clearly. It should be compared with the statue, also of wood, of Sesostris I, in which the idealization of the bodily forms is derived from the traditional abstract scheme. In this case, however, the rounded forms of the body give the work a realism in harmony with the expression of a cunning provincial nobleman emanating from the face. The balance of tension between the various parts is successfully solved by the geometrical relationship of the curves: we are, in fact, a long way from 'cubist' solutions, and it is the sphere that asserts itself. It was this sculptural conception that inspired the artists of the late Saitic period in their trend towards the archaic.

Also from the beginning of the Fifth Dynasty are the statues of Ranofer, High Priest of Ptah, in the two versions found in his tomb and now at Cairo, with and without the ritual wig (Plate 38). The face is cleverly treated, from the carefully finished eye to the slightly contemptuous lip, with a marked nobility of features incorporated in the rather broad modelling of the face. The ample wig, hanging down on both sides from a central parting, acts as a frame which sets off the face. The statue shows Ranofer standing, and although the left leg is thrust forward, in the typical walking poise, the arms are parallel with the axis of the body, giving it the structure of an automaton. This is a typical attitude, found also in the statues of the *Ka* placed on the threshold of the 'false door' to the tomb, in the act of emerging in response to the call of the living. Such statues were placed in the funerary chapel, to which the priests who officiated at the daily rites and the relatives and friends—in other words, the public—were admitted to recite the formulae of the *pert-kheru* or 'issuing of the voice', by virtue of which it was supposed that the funerary offerings, represented in the pictures, would come to life and be consumed by the *Ka*. Ranofer's is not, therefore, the classical walking pose, for in this case the left arm would be bent and carrying, as it generally does, the cane. On the contrary it is the attitude of a funerary apparition belonging to the world of the dead, characteristic of a number of works of this kind.

The fact that the image of the deceased at the 'false door' was from the very beginning designed for the public view, might lead one to suppose that in it the artist would find a stimulus to make some distinction between statuary and the decorations hidden away in the recesses of the tomb and those in the chapel to which the public had access. This, however, was not the case; the rules of the 'canon' were scrupulously observed on every occasion, and, contrary to the opinion of Junker, the evidence goes to prove that the extrinsic factor of possible 'aesthetic' criticism by chance spectators was never taken into account by the artist during the process of creation. On the contrary, the execution of the reliefs in the sepulchral chamber is sometimes superior to that of the works in

the chapel, e.g. in the *mastaba* of Mereruka at Sakkâra,
As regards the raw materials used for private statues,
plastered and painted wood and limestone held
pride of place, the latter material being more lasting
and better suited for withstanding chemical and
organic onslaughts, including the jaws of the termites.
In fact, wooden statues are often discovered that have
been irreparably mutilated. Even hard stone such as
porphyry, basalt, etc., was used for this type of
statuary, though only to a limited extent and for the
most part in later periods.

A classical pose, immortalized in the famous work
now in the Louvre, is that of the 'seated scribe'.
In the Fifth Dynasty version preserved in the Cairo
Museum, the face enframed in the neat wig is in
many ways reminiscent of the plastic structure of
the statue of Ranofer (Plate 39), with the addition
of a greater vivacity due to the inlaid crystal eye. The
aim of such types of eyes was to reproduce the actual
prototype as closely as possible, and surprisingly
realistic effects were often achieved. Generally, white
quartz and rock-crystal in a setting of copper were
used both for wooden statues and for those in stone
(Plate 40).

The private statuary of this period comprises single
figures, family groups and pseudo-groups. The
family groups often reflect the domestic harmony and
affection uniting the various members of the household. A typical attitude for wives and daughters is
the embracing of their husband or father by clasping
their arms halfway round his waist, or holding his
arm, as in the group showing Mersu-Ankh with his

two daughters, in which we find the colour convention of brown for the man and yellow ochre for
the women. In the group showing Akhi seated on
his stool with his wife and daughter at his feet, the
attitude of the women clasping the man's legs is
full of affection, despite the adherence to the system of
different proportions (Plate 41). A similar gesture
appears in the fragment of the group of Djedefrē'
from Abu Rauwâsh, in which the wife is represented
in the same proportions and attitude as in the preceding work. When we examine the statue of Akhi
more closely, his typically introspective expression
prompts the question as to 'how' Egyptian artists
were able to reconcile the characteristic individualism
of the single figures with the air of 'beatific absent-
mindedness' common to all this category of statues.
We have already mentioned one rule, that of em-
ploying the device of not representing the pupils of
the eyes, so that the eye, seen as a mere eyeball,
accentuates the idea of 'introspection'. To this must
be added another technical device which conforms
with the canon of asymmetry of the parts. In a normal
face, conceived in a moment of repose and therefore
without any signs of emotion or passion, the 'individual' tone results not only from the specific
features, but also from the fact that the two parts into
which it would be possible to divide the face by means
of a vertical line are anything but symmetrical. It is,
in fact, well known that if we reproduce the photo-
graph of a face twice in reverse, cut them in two
following a line down the centre and then place
each half by the corresponding side of the other photo,

we shall obtain two completely different portraits of the same sitter.

The Egyptian artist, aware of this principle, made the two sections of the face as similar as possible, thus obliterating the intimate characteristics of the individual. To this practice we may ascribe the 'common denominator' of the various works, independent of the features which may vary from one work to another.

'Pseudo-groups' consist of repetitions of the image of one and the same person in the same or different poses, costumes and attitudes. The number of images may range from two to considerably more. In the tomb of Irukaptah (or 'Ptahiruk') at Sakkâra, dating from the Fifth or Sixth Dynasty and also known as the tomb of the 'butchers' (Plate 42), the number of polychrome statues emerging from the niches is nine, all in the same pose. In these figures the faces show somatic variations and testify to the fashion of wearing small moustaches.

We have already mentioned the realism of the dwarf Seneb (Plate 5), but the work is not an exception. The reproduction of physical deformities was based on conceptions of realism of which enough has been said and is confirmed by the figure of Chnumhotep, a grotesque dwarf groom, dating from the early Fifth Dynasty and now in Cairo. As to bas-reliefs, the famine scenes along the 'sacred way' of Unis have a counterpart in the emaciated figures of herdsmen in the Middle Kingdom tomb at Meir, while the deformed cattle-drover in the Fifth Dynasty tomb of Ptahhotep can be compared with the figure of Iniotef, the lame comptroller of the royal household, on his stele now in London.

Old Kingdom private bas-reliefs also bear witness to the same high degree of artistic maturity as is found in sculpture. The Fifth Dynasty scene of Ti hunting in the papyrus thicket is an interesting example of the treatment of background. Amidst the play of light and shade, the papyrus stems, though arranged according to a geometrical pattern, assume a living rhythm which is transmitted to the rest of the composition (Plate 43). The motive is repeated, in another form, in the vintage scene in the tomb of Nefer-her-Ptah at Sakkâra, where the curving vines rising from the soil have bearded tops (Plate 44), producing an effect of terminal dynamism like a 'centripetal vortex'—almost like the back-surge of waves—while the peaceful occupation of the vintagers gives equilibrium to the composition. This seeking for an equilibrium lying between dynamism and stagnation can be noted in all Old Kingdom tombs; the interminable rows of men and women bearing offerings, static in their conception even though their feet are poised in the act of walking, are balanced by the scenes of activity—struggling boatmen, gymnastic exercises, dances, hunting in the desert. And the same tendency can be detected in the various portions of the composition, for example the fishermen's boat in the tomb of Kagemni (Plate 45), where the dynamism of the figure in the bow, rigid in the act of casting the net, is balanced by the fisherman holding the hooks seated in the centre of the boat, and by the oarsman, in whom, however, there is a dynamic tension due to

87

the implied effort of propulsion. A certain vivacity is also given to the scene by the fish, which are reproduced in various attitudes in the sheet of water, in accordance with a scheme of perspective that links this kind of representation with the Assyrian scenes such as that in which Sennacherib's troops are seen navigating among the reeds. One last observation must be made with regard to these bas-reliefs. In all the scenes reproducing 'typical acts', the attention to detail is carried to the point of meticulousness, and no article of clothing, no instrument or decorative element is in any way overlooked. Note, for example, the monovalve shell adorning the neck of the bull in the already-mentioned scene from the tomb of Ptahhotep (Plate 46).

During the Old Kingdom a particular category of small sculptures was evolved in which the 'servants' of the deceased were represented. During the early historical period, as has been proved by Emery's excavations at Sakkâra, it was still the custom to sacrifice to the memory of a deceased monarch a number of slaves and officials, to escort him to the next world and there to carry on the activities which had been theirs in this life. At a given moment, magic, which even in the prehistoric period had shown how the reproductions of 'things' could replace the actual articles, did away with this barbarous usage. If, it was argued, the representation of funerary offerings—meat, vegetables or furniture—could substitute the corresponding articles, why could the principle not be applied to servants as well? And in fact reproductions of them soon began to appear in private statuary. But as there was no Egyptian equivalent to the handyman or *bonne à tout faire*, each activity had to be separately represented, from the baking of bread to the brewing of beer or the woman grinding corn (Plate 47). It was this that provided the wise Ptahhotep (*c.* 2675 B.C.) with the inspiration for one of his maxims, showing the consideration in which even the humble were held: 'Do not be arrogant on account of thy learning and do not have too much confidence in thyself. Take counsel from the ignorant as well as from the wise, for the extreme limits of knowledge can never be reached and no artist has complete mastery of his art. Wise words are as hard to find as a precious emerald, yet we may hear them from a woman slave as she grinds the corn.'

Nevertheless, the slaves took an active part in the revolutionary movement that overthrew the Old Kingdom, since they were under the illusion that in order to rule it was sufficient to 'dash the children of the princes against the wall' or to wear round their own necks the jewels they had stolen from their mistresses. When the storm had subsided, the Middle Kingdom produced images of maidservants wearing no ornaments at all, for example on the sarcophagus of Queen Kawit. This, however, was a period in which the apparently immutable essential values again became a subject of controversy—the figure of the king-god, the very belief in life after death. Elsewhere we have referred to the scepticism of the banqueting songs, which exalted the pleasures of this life without worrying about the world to come, while at the same time, as so often happens in similar circumstances, diametrically opposite trends developed. When death was really imminent, even the most sceptical hastened to provide themselves with amulets, while bands of 'servants of the deceased' were installed in the tombs and an industry of model-making arose. The models were those of houses, granaries, stables, farms, animals, etc., all designed to provide the *Ka* of the deceased with every possible comfort.

The style of these models drew its inspiration from the Old Kingdom: the woman bearing offerings in the Eleventh Dynasty tomb of the noble Meketrē' (Plate 48) has a counterpart in the similar bearers in the tomb of Ti, the only difference being the more elaborate decoration of the robe, a result of the new trends in fashion, though the *allure* is absolutely identical. This, as we have already seen, was also the case with the bearers of offerings in the temple of Hatshepsut at Deir el-Bahri, which were inspired by Fifth and Sixth Dynasty models.

The strictly utilitarian occupations were not the only ones to be represented in the models of the period; more pleasing activities such as music played by competent harpers are also found.

Private iconography still wavered between imitation of the Old Kingdom, from the heritage of which the revolution had not entirely freed it, and the slavish reproductions of models inspired by royal statuary.

The Eleventh Dynasty stele of Thethi now in the British Museum shows this personage in an attitude and style absolutely identical with those of the Sixth Dynasty representation of Mereruka.

A symptom of the customs of the times can be discerned in stelae in which the deceased is shown with more than one wife, as in the case of Iniotef or Iker-ur of the Eleventh Dynasty, who have three. There was no limitation of the number of wives in Egypt during the Old Kingdom, but the trend was towards monogamy. Concubines *a latere* were accepted, but on sepulchral stelae artists generally represented only the legitimate spouse. In London we have also the stele of the Lady Khu, who insisted on having both her husbands, the equerries Si-Hathor and Si-Amun, represented thereon. Even assuming that she was a widow, the custom is anything but canonical.

The development of the so-called 'cubist' statuary experienced its golden age under the Middle Kingdom, and it is to the Twelfth Dynasty that the 'false door' of Si-Hathor, inspector of the Sudanese mines during the reign of Amenemhet II, is attributed. Here the figure no longer has the typical Old Kingdom pose, but is enclosed within the co-ordinates of a cube from which only his head emerges.

The prototype of the naophorous statue, i.e. those in which a figure is shown with a small votive chapel in front of it, is the Thirteenth Dynasty statue of the priest Iri in red quartzite, now in London. This work shows Iri with his head carefully shaved in accordance with the rules of the priesthood, holding in front of him a little votive stele bearing invocations to Anubis. This type of statuary became general during the Saitic and Persian periods, and to the latter belongs the important Vatican *naophore* showing the priest and archiater (or chief physician) Udje-har-resnet, who informs us, by means of the text incised upon his robes, of certain otherwise unknown aspects of the policy of Cambyses in Egypt.

Remote from Old Kingdom influences and almost a prelude to the New Kingdom was sculpture in wood, which also, however, avoided excessive meticulousness in minor details; see, for example, the Twelfth Dynasty head of a woman from el-Lisht—that is to say the same place where the statue of Sesostris I, also in wood, was found. The wig, fashioned separately from the head, is treated like a block, without any particular care in the execution of the accessories, though it is enlivened by golden streaks, representing the little golden tubes worn in their head-dress by fashionable ladies of the period. The artist's attention has been concentrated on the face, to which he has managed to give a note of sober refinement (Plate 49). This work can be compared with the wooden statuette, also dating from the Twelfth Dynasty, of the Lady Imeret-nebes, now at Leyden. Here too the head and wig have been treated separately, according to a technique which was evidently general. On the whole the art of the Middle Kingdom testifies, in private icono-graphy, to the survival of certain elements from the past and to a pre-knowledge of others of the future. It is thus a transitional art, reflecting the moral and political uncertainty, even if on occasions it is en-livened by flashes of originality showing that there was a desire for improvement. Under the Hyksos regime there was a complete absence of activity on the part of Egyptian artists, but during this period of constraint the germs of new tendencies ripened which were developed during the following period, in the wake of a new Egyptian empire.

The dawn of the New Kingdom reflected, even in private statuary, all the oriental desire for luxury, the meticulous care of the person as regards ornaments and elaborate robes. The family groups, which under the Old Kingdom had stressed the human motive by expressing the reality of affectionate feelings, were now suffocated beneath a formal elegance, for example in the Eighteenth Dynasty group of Iri-nefer and Aper in the British Museum, or that of Thai and Naia in Cairo, with its typically reserved air (Plate 50). The classic gesture of the wife clasping her husband's waist loses all its emotional intensity and is reduced to a mere pragmatic pose based on a code of good manners. The identity of the features shows a marked trend towards idealization of forms, the inevitable consequence of stylization.

The 'servants' of the deceased, so numerous and varied under the Middle Kingdom, now assume the aspect of mummy-like statuettes, and become the *ushabti* in faïence, wood or limestone, or even in metal, on which is inscribed the text of the sixth chapter of 'The Book of the Dead', that made its first appearance about this time.

The name *ushabti* or *shauabti* is probably derived from the word *ushab* = 'to reply', in reference to the text, which runs as follows:

'O thou *ushabti*—if I should be called or obliged to accomplish any task among those that must be accomplished in the world to come—see that the decision fall upon thee instead of upon me, and this always, whether the task be reaping the fields, filling the canals with water, or moving the sand.'

The text also included the reply of the *ushabti*: 'In truth I am here and will come wherever you may command me.'

These types of 'servants' replaced the various categories of the preceding periods, during which hundreds and even thousands of them were represented in the tombs of kings and nobles.

Private bas-reliefs followed lines of development parallel to those of royal reliefs. In fact, the first courtiers' tombs were decorated by the same artists who executed the royal bas-reliefs, and we cannot therefore expect to find any substantial differences. A characteristic, however, is the supreme elegance of the drawing and the infinite attention paid to details, both of which qualities are displayed in the tomb of the Vizier Ramose (Plate 51). A breath of spirituality also pervades the reign of Amenophis III, and in the tomb of Kheruef, which we have already mentioned several times, a group of female dancers is shown performing a 'sacred dance' in the presence of the king on the occasion of a jubilee festival (Plate 52). The rhythm, despite the strange poses of the figures, is restrained and measured, and almost makes us forget the attention paid to the coiffures. This restraint is a quality which we shall seek in vain during the following dynasty. Take, for example, the funerary dance in a Nineteenth Dynasty bas-relief from Sakkâra (Plate 53): here there is an attempt to achieve calligraphical effect in the details, an insistence on the part of the artist on the anatomy of the figures as seen through the transparent draperies. Not that this bas-relief lacks life. On the contrary, it appears as if pervaded with frenzy and we seem almost to hear the rhythmical beat of the tambourines and castanets, in tune with the movements of the musicians. Perspective is achieved by means of a partial overlapping of the personages. The two young dancers with castanets are shown in front of a girl playing a tambourine, who in her turn precedes another. Whereas the royal bas-relief at Medinet Habu shows the troops in lateral perspective, thus giving a comprehensive view of the soldiers in the various ranks, here the perspective is achieved by superimposition of the figures, which emerge—from the waist upwards—above those who precede them. This bas-relief is also interesting because it illustrates another characteristic of the period: the extreme care in the rendering of the hands and feet with their elongated lines.

Of Saitic art we have already spoken when dealing with royal iconography. It produced copies of Old Kingdom models with an accentuation of old age and ugliness, reducing the stone to the smoothness of a mirror without contriving to convey any message. The stylization of expression and gestures eliminated every trace of emotion. It was the triumph of technical skill, of 'craftsmanship' apart from all other considerations. To this period belong the representations of personages afflicted with gynaecomastitis, who also seem to be in complete contradiction to the traditional aesthetic 'canon' (Plate 6 and Plate E).

CHAPTER SIX

Painting

WHEN we turn to the study of Egyptian painting, the question at once arises whether this form of art, like sculpture, was also 'conditioned by Death'; whether, that is to say, it represents nothing but a technique bound up with the magico-religious finalism we have already had occasion to mention.

The answer can be both affirmative and negative. In fact, almost all the examples that have come down to us were found in tombs, and there can be no doubt that in such cases they fulfilled the same function as the bas-reliefs, and we have already mentioned the close relationship between these two manifestations of art. But that does not exclude the possibility that a form of painting 'for the living' may have existed at the same time, the function of which was mainly decorative. Unfortunately the cities of Egypt have long been mingled with the dust of the desert, though a few elements, sporadic though they may be, confirm our assertion. On carved sarcophagi of the Old Kingdom we already find reproductions of the façade of a 'palace' with its ornaments and colouring, while fragments from the walls and pavements of the palace of Amenophis III at Thebes and of the royal residence at Amarna show that domestic frescoes existed and that, to a far greater extent than sculpture

LIST OF COLOUR PLATES

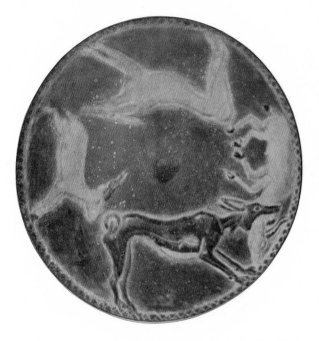

PLATE A. "Magic disc" with hunting scene. From Sakkâra. First
Dynasty. Green steatite with alabaster incrustations.
Diameter $2\frac{1}{2}$ inches; 6·5 cm. *Cairo, Museum.*

PLATE B. "Magic disc" with birds in a trap. From Sakkâra. First Dynasty. Limestone and steatite with alabaster incrustations. Diameter 3⅛ inches; 8 cm. *Cairo, Museum.*

PLATE C. Horse and rider in painted wood. Early Eighteenth Dynasty.
Height 12 inches; 30.5 cm. *New York, Metropolitan Museum.*

PLATE D. Bust in stuccoed and painted wood from the tomb of King
Tutankhamun. Original lifesize. *Cairo, Museum.*

PLATE E. Prince Harwa. Granite statue from Karnak. Twenty-fifth Dynasty. Height 18 inches; 45 cm. *Cairo, Museum.*

Plate F. Queen Nefertari playing draughts. Nineteenth Dynasty.
Fresco from her tomb in Thebes.

PLATE G. Painter's sketches. New Kingdom. *Cairo, Museum.*

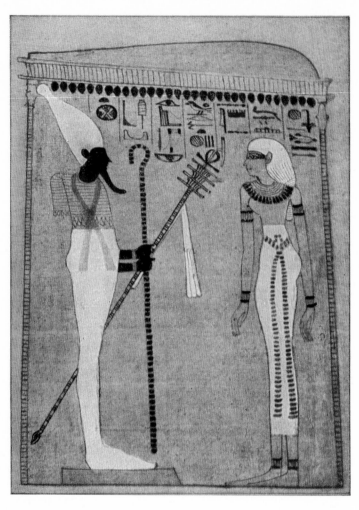

PLATE H. Vignette on papyrus, from the "Book of the Dead" of the priestess Nesikhonsu. Twenty-first Dynasty. *Cairo, Museum.*

PLATE I. Faience bowl. New Kingdom. Diameter 6½ inches; 16.5 cm.
Turin, Museum.

PLATE J. Golden mask of the mummy of Tutankhamun.
Height 19¾ inches; 50 cm. *Cairo, Museum.*

and bas-reliefs, painting, like architecture, served to render the houses of the living more pleasing and attractive, in particular the royal residences and the houses of the nobility.

Nevertheless, in view of the scarcity of examples of this particular kind, we have to restrict the meaning of the term 'Egyptian painting' to funerary works, i.e. the adornment of tombs. Despite this limitation, however, there are numerous points of contact between the art intended for the dead and that destined for the living, since both the stylistic rules and the technical system of perspective and proportions were identical. A greater freedom in the choice of subjects may perhaps have been granted to the decorators of palaces, and this is confirmed by certain extant items, though these all date from the Amarna period. This, however, was a period of revolution and the items cannot, therefore, be considered as having a general validity.

According to Pliny the Elder, the Egyptians invented painting six thousand years before the Greeks, starting from drawings—'umbra hominis lineis circumducta'—the shadows of men traced by lines.

And in actual fact, when we study the human figures reproduced pictorially in the various tombs, the impression we receive is that they are precisely 'coloured shadows'. Far removed from the modern idea of colouring, which by means of an infinite number of gradations creates relief, plasticity and depth, the Egyptian painter projected a simple silhouette on to the basic plane and coloured it in only one shade.

This chromatic 'mono-tonality' cannot, however, be ascribed to a presumed 'primitivism', for even in the remotest prehistoric eras the artists who painted on rocks had shown their ability to produce pictorial compositions rich in nuances. This would involve having to speak of a 'regression' in comparison with Magdalenian art!

It is, on the contrary, necessary to remember what has already been said about the functional nature of Egyptian funerary art. It was a question of creating 'archetypes' and thus, in essence, an idealization of reality. Colour, and for that matter the figure itself, were thus purely conventional and symbolic. The figures of women were depicted in yellow ochre to distinguish them from the brick-red figures of men, not because those were their real colours, but because they were thus conceived as prototypes of the entity 'woman'. Similarly, a Negro was depicted in dark brown and an Asiatic in yellowish tones, and if the scene comprised a number of figures standing side by side, convention ruled that light-coloured figures should alternate with dark, so as to create a kind of relief by means of contrast.

At this point, to make matters clearer, we will summarize the salient characteristics of Egyptian painting, in order to stress the points of contact between this branch of art and the sister-art of bas-relief:

(*a*) In the case of human figures, constant application of the law of 'frontality' and of the geometrical canon. An inscription on the temple at Edfu, referring to an inventory of the temple library, informs us that on one of the shelves was the 'Book of Prescriptions for mural painting and of the proportions to be given to the figures'. And Diodorus, on this subject, says: 'They divided the whole body into twenty-one parts and a quarter and from this established the structure of man.'

These canonical rules were applied with greater severity to the tombs of sovereigns than they were to those of private individuals. Frequently, in fact, provincial art, or that which characterized determined periods of social and political unrest, disregarded, at all events to a certain extent, the strict details of the canon, substituting for them a coarse and careless execution.

(*b*) Realistic treatment of figures and details, but systematic conventionalism in the colouring, except in simple sketches, in which only the outlines of the figures are indicated (cf. the 'female mourners' in the tomb of Haremhab).

(*c*) The artist is given freedom to modify the pre-established themes. In other words, variations of the same motive.

(*d*) Execution of subjects representing 'typical acts' in Egyptian life.

From the above it can be seen that we ought to speak of 'coloured drawings' rather than of 'painting'. From the earliest historical period, in fact, the Egyptians displayed a marked talent for drawing and perfect calligraphy, but they never succeeded in freeing themselves from the subservience to forms, and even the 'explosions' of colour which occasionally lend animation to the scenes are nothing but deliberately calculated constructing without any real spontaneity.

The most evident point of contact between painting and bas-relief was obviously the first stage—common to both of them—namely the drawing. The two branches of art are also linked by the similarity of the subjects, since the aim behind their execution was the same. Moreover, painted bas-reliefs were executed even during the Old Kingdom period, thus providing another proof of the intimate connexion with painting.

In this latter case the various stages of the artist's work are clearly visible, just as they are in bas-reliefs, since nearly all the tombs were left 'unfinished', and we find progressive sketches of the figures with traces of geometrical signs, the grid on the background, areas only partly coloured, etc.

When speaking of the analogous custom in tombs adorned with bas-reliefs and sculptures, we suggested —though only as a hypothesis—an explanation of the motives which may have been the reason for this practice. Nevertheless, one cannot ignore the opinion expressed by some scholars on this point.

It is usually accepted that almost all the tombs show some signs of incompleteness. The 'paradox' consists in the fact that the really finished works constitute exceptions, 'and even when all the walls are decorated down to the last line, at least one element is left in the state of a sketch'.

All this is in perfect accord with the actual state of affairs. Somewhat less convincing, perhaps, is the proposed explanation: 'Undoubtedly the reason for this could have been the laziness attributed to the inhabitants of hot climates and the premature death of the patrons.'

From the psychological point of view it would be really interesting to study the effects of a congenital laziness which for thousands of years caused artists to stop working when they were on the point of finishing the 'last sketch'. And all that, be it noted, without any protest on the part of the client because the work had been left unfinished and without any demand that the work must be terminated before the artists received payment! The explanation of this strange attitude might be provided by the second hypothesis—the premature death of the patrons. From the biological standpoint it would be equally interesting to analyse the causes of the premature deaths of all the patrons, since, as already stated, the incompleteness is almost universal and really finished tombs are rare exceptions. If we discard such interpretations, we can affirm without hesitation that, whatever may have been the motive underlying this practice, it was the result of a deliberate decision, in other words a volitive, not a casual, act, which for the very reason that it was constantly repeated in tombs must necessarily have been based on a magico-religious, finalistic conception. I would remark at this point that in ancient Peru—as has been proved by archaeological finds—it was customary to bury with the deceased an incompletely embroidered cloth, which, in accordance with Peruvian belief, would be finished by the deceased in the next world.

Returning to the question of successive stages of execution, we may assume that, once the dimensions had been established and the necessary data collected from the tomb prepared by the architects, drawings of the scenes would first be executed to scale on the equivalents of 'cartoons' and submitted to the proprietor for his approval. The latter might demand that formal alterations be made in accordance with his own tastes: for example, an army general would insist on scenes of a military character; a vizier would wish to see himself represented while holding an audience; a 'scribe of the fields' while measuring land, and so on.

The background might be either the natural wall of the tomb, if this had been hewn out of the rock, lightly coated with stucco or plaster, or else a supporting wall of Nile clay mixed with straw and coated with several layers of plaster. The painting was executed in tempera with mineral colours dissolved in water and by means of a gum-like 'medium'. The extraordinary brightness of these works must undoubtedly be attributed for the most part to the exceptional climatic conditions, but it is impossible to overlook the existence of a profound knowledge of 'technique' in the strict sense of the term. The palette was somewhat limited as regards choice of colours, with a definite predominance of ochres and burnt sienna. Green and blue were equivalents of each other, i.e. they were considered as 'tonal' variations of the same colour, while the sea, which is a synthesis of the two, was known by only one name—*wadj wr*, the 'Great Green'. White was used especially for clothing and, during certain periods, for the background itself.

The wall, after being coated with plaster, presented a smooth and easy surface and on it were executed, in red ink, the geometrical divisions which facilitated the transfer of the sketch previously drawn to scale, while, probably under the supervision of a 'master', the assistants reproduced the various compositions on the walls. Since these compositions had been created in conformity with strict geometrical rules, they could not possibly reveal diversity of authorship, unlike certain Renaissance compositions in churches, where the work, likewise under the guidance of a 'master', was entrusted to various hands. Naturally there are exceptions which may comprise whole compositions, and Roeder, in his attempt to demonstrate the originality of certain Egyptian artists, claims to have recognized two different hands at Bet el-Wāli and Dakka, one adhering closely to tradition and the other showing signs of an original style.

As regards the execution of paintings in tombs, the method of illuminating the apartments in which the artists had to work remains a mystery. The light coming from the entrance, and this only in surface tombs, would not have been sufficient, while the problem of the subterranean chambers remains unsolved. The lamps that have come down to us would have been quite inadequate for this purpose and in any case could not have provided the minimum of lighting required for decorating high walls, on which the smallest detail is traced with a high degree of technical perfection and in a miniature-like style that would present difficulties even if executed in broad daylight. Nor can we accept the hypothesis of the use of resinous torches, since these would certainly have quickly consumed the scanty supply of oxygen in the chambers and thus prevented the continuation of the work; moreover, torches would certainly have left traces of smoke on the ceilings, whereas they are completely free from such traces and have preserved for us very delicate ornaments. At the present stage of our knowledge we can only point out that this problem exists and hope that future discoveries may provide the solution.

The rules of perspective followed in the composition of the various scenes are the same as those governing the execution of bas-reliefs. When the work is divided into horizontal strips, the lowest is always conceived as being the nearest to the spectator, while the tradition of hierarchical proportions implies the classic representation of the personages with their stature varying according to their individual importance. Apart from this, the figures in the various rows are generally of the same, and not of diminishing, size. The convention whereby the lowest row represented the point nearest to the spectator was therefore limited to the idea of spatial depth. An interesting exception to this rule is to be found in a scene in the tomb of Nebamun, dating from the early years of the New Kingdom, in which three peasants with sacks of grain on their shoulders are reproduced in diminishing size on three successive planes; this, however, was just an experiment which remained an isolated case.

Although it is impossible to speak of any real 'evolution' in Egyptian painting, we can nevertheless recognize various styles which were, at least in part, the fruit of definite epochs. In fact, if, by 'evolution', we understand a progressive stage in any kind of development, characterized by a new feeling or a new way of interpreting and seeing, though still closely bound up with the preceding period, then we have to admit that no such thing occurred in Egyptian painting. Even the Amarna revolution, as we shall see in due course, did not in any sense represent an 'evolution', but rather a 'break'. There were, however, stylistic variations, influenced in particular by fashion and by the social and political trends of the moment; there is evidence of these throughout all the historical periods, and notably during the New Kingdom era.

If we wish to gain a synthetic, panoramic view of the 'history of style' in Egyptian painting, excluding the pre-dynastic period, of which, however, we reproduce one example—the wall-painting at Hieraconpolis (Plate 2)—we must first of all examine the rare specimens dating from the Old Kingdom.

From the Fourth Dynasty we have examples which can already be described as 'classical'. This was, in fact, the 'golden age' of the arts, and even if painting was used to a much smaller extent than the bas-relief at this time, it did not escape the influence of Memphis, where the workshops produced the greatest masterpieces of the period. The famous 'Geese of Mēdūm' from the tomb of Itet (Plate 54) reveal at the same time a mastery of draughtsmanship, a taste for colour, a sense of reality and a geometrical rhythm in the composition. As regards the colours, these are not just casually chosen or in any sense 'abstract'. Gaillard had no difficulty in identifying among these figures the four principal breeds of Egyptian geese, and the painter has been strictly realistic.

In the tomb of Neferma'et dating from the same period, the artist experimented with a new technique: instead of applying the colour directly to the wall, he carefully carved out the figures and then filled them with a coloured paste. The purpose of this technique is clearly explained in an inscription on the wall: 'They will never fade!' Unfortunately, at many points the colour has broken away *en bloc*, thus contradicting the artist's rash assertion, but at the same time allowing us to make an accurate study of the technical method of execution.

The Egyptians' marked feeling for calligraphy is revealed from the very beginning, as can be seen in 'The Birds' from the Fifth Dynasty tomb of Nefer-her-Ptah in Sakkâra. The style is that of miniatures with an oriental tendency (Plate 55), the composition is full of rhythm and charm, and attention has been paid to realistic details and general equilibrium, so that there is no sense of confusion, despite the fact that the wall has been crowded with figures to an incredible extent.

Under the Sixth Dynasty the first signs of a certain decadence appear, harbingers of the subsequent social upheaval. The style becomes careless, almost provincial in appearance and therefore quite un-justifiable in the necropolis of Memphis. The scenes of slaughter in the tomb of Irukaptah, although they belong to a preceding epoch, already reveal decadent trends, even if in the rendering of funerary offerings the artist frees himself to a certain extent from the carelessness of the other paintings and achieves genuine chromatic harmony—vases in alternating colours, offerings of animals and vegetables which balance one another, polychrome hieroglyphs in tune with the rest of the composition.

Nevertheless, most of the Old Kingdom tombs are decorated with bas-reliefs which, even if painted, cannot, technically speaking, be considered as 'paintings'. In any case, the rare examples of these enable us to trace the development of this period: the starting-point was already 'classical' and therefore completely mature at the time of the Fourth Dynasty, which, together with the Fifth, constituted the zenith of art. During this phase the miniaturistic style predominated, with a continual search for 'reality' as regards both form and colour (especially in the rendering of animals, whereas in that of human beings the chromatic 'convention' is already evident). Under the Sixth Dynasty came decadence: the draughtsmanship became careless, the clumsy application of the colours accentuated the crudely realistic and 'provincial' factors.

From the Middle Kingdom we have the tombs of various nomarchs at Beni-Hasan, in a somewhat precarious state owing to the patina that has formed on them. The Old Kingdom taste for miniatures still survives and is still seen in a picture of 'Birds on an acacia tree', combined with a certain calligraphical trend. But at the same time there is a greater freedom of line: two wrestlers are seen gripping each other closely (Plate 56), while a 'Woman spinning' twists the fingers of her hand holding the bobbin. These are rather coarse figures, both with flowing lines. The dancing-girls in the Twelfth Dynasty tomb of

Antefoker show a certain rhythm in the composition, reminiscent, as regards the faces, of the figures on the sarcophagus of Queen Kawit dating from the same period (Plate 24). On the whole, therefore, although care is still taken at this time in the drawing of animals (cf. the bas-relief of the 'Weeping Cow'), the human figures are less accurate, especially in the execution of the faces, which, aesthetically speaking, are not beautiful. It is a period still under the influence of the traumatic shock of the preceding upheaval. The art of painting is to a certain extent trying to find its feet and wavers between the remnants of a spiritually shattered tradition—from which, however, it does not succeed in freeing itself completely—and the search for new forms lacking in genuine inspiration.

It was not until another period of restrictions arrived that the germs of the stylistic trends characteristic of the beginning of the new era began to ferment. Unlike the First Intermediate period, which, for internal reasons affecting all values, marked the end of the Old Kingdom, this 'second period' strengthened the cohesion of the various Egyptian forces against the invaders. In the first period the complete destruction of traditional 'feeling', and the mass poisoning of men's minds by class hatred, made it impossible for the germs of art to mature, but the same cannot be said of the second period, when the suffering inflicted on a whole people by a common evil which struck impartially at all classes helped to bring about a renaissance of national values. In the political sphere the renaissance first declared itself in the war of liberation and later in the policy of imperial expansion, while in the field of art it resulted in a return to the antique, as if moral support were being sought for the national aspirations. And the monumental conceptions which had been eliminated under the Middle Kingdom also reappeared, achieving extreme forms of expression such as the 'Colossi of Memnon' and the temple at Abu Simbel.

But the New Kingdom was above all the period of the greatest development in the art of painting. Thebes became the capital of the kingdom, in spiritual opposition to Sakkâra; and painting on flat surfaces regained supremacy over the bas-reliefs of the Old Kingdom even if these had been polychrome. Tombs were hewn out of the rock in remote recesses, to conceal them from the avid searchings of robbers and protect them from the hands of the mob. The sovereign and his courtiers had learned their lesson through the bitter experience of the dark periods of social strife, and a dramatic account of the events of that time has survived: 'A thing that had never happened before: the King was carried away by the poor. That which the pyramid concealed became empty. . . .'

The beginning of the New Kingdom, with its 'return to the sources', was characterized, in painting as well, by a return to archaism. The choice of subject-matter was influenced by religious conceptions and, starting with that of Tuthmosis I, the royal hypogea were adorned with scenes from the sacred texts, foremost among which was 'The Book of what is in the Netherworld', telling the story of the sun-god's nocturnal voyage and his 'descent to the nether regions'. In private tombs episodes from

civilian life and agricultural scenes were juxtaposed
in the series known as that of the 'typical acts', and
new 'experiments' were added. The tomb of the
Vizier Rekhmerē' is famous for its surprising abundance of scenes illustrating the salient aspects of his
life. Side by side with the 'typical acts' we find narrative elements: his investiture in the office of vizier,
the arrival of foreign vassals, an audience in the
palace. The banquet scene shows a maidservant seen
from the back, while other personages are represented
in profile, the law of frontality being thus abandoned.
As we have said, these were 'experiments' and thus
had no normative value, but they sometimes revealed
signs of external influences, as in the hunting scene
in the same tomb with its strange 'flying beasts'
(Plate 57). These are the animals generally found in
such scenes (dogs, antelopes, etc.), but here they are
shown with all four feet off the ground, thus giving
the impression that they are flying through space.
This is clearly an Aegean influence, as is proved by
comparison with the frescoes in the palace of Tiryns,
in which 'flying beasts' are to be seen (Plate 58).
Even if these attempts proved abortive, they reveal
the spiritual tendency of the artists of that time,
anxiously searching for new ideas in perspective.
It should be noted that in normal praxis the only
figures shown facing to the front were those of
prisoners or dead enemies. On the other hand, a fine
fragment from an Eighteenth Dynasty Theban tomb,
now in the British Museum, shows two musicians
seen direct from the front, who are accompanying
two female dancers (Plate 59). The scene thus assumes

a very different spatial value for the spectator. And the fleeing hare in the tomb of Userhat, a royal scribe during the reign of Amenophis II, is a snapshot, transferred to the wall of a tomb, of an immobilized 'dynamic' act, while in the same tomb we have the pathetic scene of the fox dying among the bushes (Plate 60). Here the artist infringes the canon by inserting a breath of human pity, and the animated rendering of the hunt seems to be interrupted by this detail of the dying animal. 'Extemporaneous' subjects of this kind, which made it possible to introduce vivid and palpitating details into the now well-worn repertoire of everyday scenes and identical motives, can also be seen in the tomb of Menna, with its profusion of agricultural scenes (Plate 61). These show the typical phases of the harvest, the threshing of grain, etc., but the artist cannot resist the temptation to describe, with a faint underlying irony, two 'episodes' of rural life. While the men are carrying away the ears of corn in a basket, two young women gleaners are having a violent quarrel over the division of what is left; one of them seizes the other by the hair and tugs at it, at the same time trying to thrust away the wrist of her rival who has grabbed the major part of the booty; one of the women is kneeling and the other is half upright, and this gives a certain dynamic tension to the scene. In the lower register, two other female gleaners are being much more polite to each other: a sharp thorn has pierced the foot of one of them and the other is trying to extract it. One would expect to find such free attitudes in a sketch-book rather than on the walls of a tomb, and they were later copied by Saitic art. In the tomb of Nakht, contemporary with the preceding tomb, two vintagers are shown picking grapes from a pergola. The grapes in the hand of the first man are light and airy, as if they weighed practically nothing, while the vine itself seems to be lightened by the contrast between the colours of the grapes and the leaves.

Very frequent are the hunting scenes, especially with boomerangs in papyrus thickets, the hunter being usually accompanied by his wife and children. This is the case both with Nakht and with the owner of another tomb, a scene from which is now preserved in London. In this a 'hunting cat' is also shown, seizing three birds at once with its claws (Plate 62). The Egyptians, alone among ancient peoples, succeeded in training cats to such an extent that they could take them out hunting, just as we take dogs today. Usually the background of hunting scenes in papyrus thickets consists only partially of vertical lines, in order to allow the upper part of the hunter's body to emerge, which it does not do in Old Kingdom reliefs. In the tomb of Amenemhet, a nobleman who lived in the reign of Tuthmosis III during the early years of the New Kingdom, the stems of the papyri are very high in the scene showing the boatman about to tie up his boat.

The luxury and profusion which characterized the 'imperial' periods are reflected in the frequent banqueting scenes, in which noble ladies are often represented sniffing at flowers, while maids pour perfumes over their hands, or gracefully adjust their trinkets and coiffures (Plate 63). These maids, usually very young, are depicted with adipose folds on their bellies as they bend over to attend to their mistresses, and the artists seem to linger over these folds—a stylistic tendency which is also noticeable in the above-mentioned scene of the quarrelling gleaners in the tomb of Menna.

Banqueting scenes are found, together with other subjects, in the tombs of Djehuti and Djeserkaraseneb—mutilated by vandals, but some of the stolen fragments have been traced—and also in the tomb of Nebamun. The sumptuousness of the clothing and the attention paid to the wigs are in accordance with the tendencies of the time which we noted when discussing the sculptures. But there is also much insistence on funeral scenes with weeping mourners, and the theme of the bereaved widow is fully exploited. In the reign of Amenophis III there was another revival of 'classicism', with a feeling for harmony of line and stylistic elegance. The 'experiments' typical of the preceding epoch are rejected in favour of the canonical rules, adapted to the new form of conscience; in human figures, the canon is respected as regards dimensions and the alternation of colours in the case of processions, for example in the funeral cortège in the tomb of Ramose, but the animals display suppleness in their gait, a good example being the enormous bull in a mural painting from the royal palace.

The Amarna interlude will be described in another chapter, in which we shall also deal with the period immediately following it, when surviving traces of its influence were still visible. In the Ramesside period painting, like bas-reliefs, was deprived of all its strength. The tomb of Queen Nefertari, wife of Ramesses II, is a good example. Elegant clothing and trappings, delicacy of features—one could repeat here what has already been said about the bas-reliefs of Sethos I. The virus of decadence, which developed during the period of greatest national glory, now begins to influence the descending curve (Plate F). In the necropolis of Deir el-Medîneh, a favourite burial-place of craftsmen, the subterranean tomb of Sennedjem deserves mention for its scenes relating to life in the netherworld as well as for those of agricultural labours (Plate 64). There are frequent representations of the two sacred trees—the sycamore and the palm—which flourished on the banks of the river. Deir el-Medîneh, inhabited by a community of artists and minor functionaries, was also the birthplace of a particular genre of art which has been preserved for us amidst shapeless heaps of debris. These are the *ostraka* or potsherds, which provided artists with the equivalent of the pages of an album for sketches and pictorial experiments: on them we see human figures, priests, girls dancing and swimming, and animals, all remarkably lifelike (Plate G). Here the artist could try his hand with far greater freedom than on the walls of tombs and temples, and he spontaneously resorted to satire. The conception of the netherworld and the profusion of funerary ornaments tend to make us forget that the Egyptians were a vivacious people with a keen sense of humour, keener, perhaps, than that of any other people. A large portion of their literature consists of 'love lyrics', while the *ostraka* are full of flashes of wit. A favourite theme is the eternal rivalry between mice and cats, the latter being depicted while acting as nurses or maidservants to the former (Plate 65), while other cats are seen herding geese and a lion is shown playing chess with a unicorn. Elsewhere we find a fox playing a flute while a goat dances: all these look like illustrations to the stories of a contemporary La Fontaine, and it is, in fact, quite possible that they were intended to illustrate fables. The 'Swimming Girl' in the museum at Turin (Plate 66) is a graceful work, similar to the analogous figures on cosmetic spoons, with which we shall deal in the chapter devoted to 'The Minor Arts'. On the whole, a study of the *ostraka* serves to integrate that of the classical representations in tombs and offers new visions of the 'immediacy of expression' which is so rare in Egyptian painting. We must not, therefore, underestimate the debt we owe the investigators of that remote period, the products of which, rescued from heaps of rubbish, are a valuable aid to any attempt to understand the visual aesthetics of the ancient Egyptians.

We have mentioned satirical papyri. When dealing with painting that has been described as 'coloured drawing', we must not forget to mention the 'miniatures' executed on papyri (Plate H). Under the New Kingdom the popularity of funerary texts such as 'The Book of the Dead', 'The Book of what is in the Netherworld', etc., gave rise to the production of papyrus scrolls inscribed and adorned with miniatures, which were naturally designed to appeal to all readers. After the beautifully decorated editions with elegantly executed hieroglyphs came abbreviated, popular editions. Many of the scenes painted on the walls of tombs were reproduced on papyri—the funeral cortège, the ceremony of the 'Opening of the Mouth', the spirits inhabiting the world to come, the fields of *Iaru* which the deceased would cultivate, and the 'Judgement' of souls before Osiris. These papyri are thus useful aids to the study, not only of the text, but also of the style, often very similar to that of mural paintings. In this genre of art, to a greater extent than in others, the Egyptian artist expressed the maximum degree of his talent as a born draughtsman, sometimes achieving a very high standard of quality. And just as, in another field, we are astonished by the primitiveness of the instruments used for the creation of works of sculpture, so too are we puzzled and moved to admiration by the thin reeds and simple little pots used for grinding and melting mineral colours. But the Egyptians had a feeling for art in their blood and could make the most primitive instruments conform to their will. Sometimes seven generations of the same family bore the title of 'Director of the Painters of Amun'. Love for their art enabled them to mix with the colours of their palettes a little of that sun which they worshipped as a divinity, which blessed the soil of Egypt with its rays. Despite the passage of five thousand years the brilliance of these paintings has remained unimpaired and can still make an appeal to our feelings.

CHAPTER SEVEN

Amarna art

To THE reign of Amenophis IV—Akhenaten—we devote a separate chapter in this book because it was a separate chapter in the history of Egypt and Akhenaten was one of the most peculiar figures known to history. He was completely averse to the original Egyptian spirit and in fact directly opposed to it; he was a kind of strange tumour in the body of the Pharaonic State, on the conceptions of which he inflicted a far graver blow than the preceding 'intermediate periods', and the doctrine he proclaimed died with him, for he left neither proselytes nor followers. And even if a certain surviving influence can be detected in his immediate successors, the Ramesside era, at all events in matters of art, ignored the Amarna interlude and returned to the traditional canon, though by this time it had been emptied of all its essential content.

When discussing the plastic arts, we compared the bas-relief of Sethos I with a 'beautiful Baroque watch with a broken spring'. If we try to identify the individual who inserted the destructive instrument into this delicate mechanism, there is only one answer —Amenophis IV.

Nevertheless, a serious study of his reign must necessarily take into account the historical precedents and causes, even if indirect, that led to the rise of the new phenomenon.

Generally speaking, the tendency is to attach too much importance to the figure of the schismatic king, whose grotesque iconography seems to exercise a morbid fascination, and to assign a subordinate rôle to the political and social influences of the time and to the part played by various personalities, among whom the Queen Mother Tiy was pre-eminent.

Even the supposed 'originality' of the monotheistic tendency attributed to Amenophis IV cannot survive a serious critical examination. Drioton, among other writers, has shown that 'an impressive number of witnesses prove that, at the beginning of the Old Kingdom, the Egyptians already had a notion of philosophy similar to our own: namely that of a god, not specifically named (and consequently conceived as the only god), the controller of events, the providence of human beings, the judge and retributor of good and bad actions'.

Nether Wa, or the 'one and only god', was the formula describing the Demiurge, one in his essence, but who assumed different names in the various theological systems. The gods were merely the personifications of his attributes. Thus it was said: 'He is Rē', who created the gods by naming his members.'

Logically, this monotheistic conception was confined to the cultured class, while the mass of the people preferred to worship one of the 'personifications' of the god instead of an abstract conception of him.

Having thus conceded the pre-existence of a monotheistic conception, let us cast a glance over the political and social background of the period in question. We have already seen that the godfathers, so to speak, of the New Kingdom were the priests of Amun, who was originally a Theban god and later achieved national status. The extremely powerful priesthood of this deity found an important ally in Queen Hatshepsut, whom they may even have used as a pawn in their subtle political manœuvres.

To obtain an idea of the power of this priesthood, we must remember that the High Priest of Rē' at Heliopolis bore the title of 'Second Priest of Amun at Thebes'. The old solar doctrine with Rē' as Demiurge had been theologically re-elaborated by combining the two divine figures in that of Amun-Rē'.

During the reign of Amenophis III, father of the schismatic king, there developed, side by side with the State religion, but in a clandestine form, the cult of Aten, which had its origins in Heliopolis, the biblical On. We do not know what part was played in religious questions by the Hyksos minorities who had remained in a state of servitude after the defeat of their dominant caste. Aten, which can be phonetically related to the Syrian *Adon* = 'Lord', already existed as a word during the Middle Kingdom, and in its narrower etymological meaning denoted the 'solar disc' in the physical sense. Obviously, the priests of Amun could not tolerate the rise of religious tendencies of a different nature, but despite this the religion of Aten was not banned during the reign of Amenophis III. Hypothetically, the reason for this could be identified with the protection accorded to the cult by Queen Tiy, the wife of Amenophis III, who gradually supplanted her husband in the government of the country. A woman of exceptional energy and strong will, she can be compared, as a figure, with Queen Hatshepsut. Tiy's protection of the cult of Aten may have been due to her origin, which—though far from clear—was certainly not Egyptian and may have included strains of Asiatic blood. This might also serve to explain the conflict between the queen and the priests of Amun, who viewed with suspicion the growing political influence of a personage who was so definitely anti-Egyptian.

The very flourishing commercial relations with the Aegean had already influenced the arts by introducing new ideas of form such as the 'flying beasts' in the tomb of Rekhmerē', of which we have already spoken. Scenes showing Cretan tribute-payers were reproduced in tombs in the days of Hatshepsut, Tuthmosis III, Amenophis II and Rekhmerē'. But during the reign of Amenophis III there occurred the destruction of the Minoan regime as a result of the sacking of Knossos and other Cretan cities. The exodus of the survivors, many of whom must have been artists and craftsmen, obviously tended towards the hospitable land of Egypt. A flourishing Cretan colony was thus established on Egyptian soil.

Amenophis III did not enjoy good health and it was in vain that the king of Mitanni repeatedly sent him the miraculous healing statue of Ishtar. Many years after the marriage between Amenophis III and the autocratic Queen Tiy, a son was born, who shortly afterwards succeeded to the throne and to whom—in deference to the national god—the name of Amenophis = 'Amun is in peace', was given, the fourth of the dynasty.

The figure of the new sovereign is very interesting from the medical point of view. Professor P. Ghalioungui has made a close study of this subject and has been able to diagnose that Amenophis IV suffered from a congenital organic weakness, a destructive form of tuberculosis, manifest signs of hyperpituaritism, and probably from hypogonadism, while E. Snorrason stressed the fact that the sovereign probably also suffered from acromegaly (Plate 67).

It is therefore easy to understand how the influence of Queen Tiy found fertile soil in a physically degenerate being, whose epileptic tendencies, however, might have made him appear to be 'godlike', a 'prophet' of some new faith. And it is in fact in its prophetical aspect that the Aten schism exploded with the greatest virulence. Until that time, the theology of the Pharaonic regime, though readjusted as the result of previous social upheavals, had had its roots in the idea that the king was the incarnation of the divine solar principle (Rē') and at the same time the symbol of Horus, the son of Osiris and avenger of his father. The doctrine of Aten discarded Osiris completely, which practically means that it discarded the whole of the netherworld, and exalted the value of the cosmic symbol in its purely physical sense, and Amenophis IV proclaimed himself the 'Prophet of the Living Sun', the 'Only Being that can communicate the Divine Doctrine'. The name of the new divinity was defined as the 'Heat that is in Aten', and subsequently altered to the 'Fire emanating from Aten'. This was a deification of the vital warmth emanating from the sun, and the mistake is commonly made of stressing the presumed spirituality in the interpretation of the conception of Aten. In reality, we have here to do with a kind of naturism, perhaps sublimated, which makes the sun, or rather its heat, deprived of its previous symbolical religious attributes, the only source of life. The Egyptian equivalent of 'god' in the abstract sense is *Nether*, which is used as a designation for divinity in general. Amenophis IV prohibited the use of this term and had it deleted wherever it had been engraved. If, therefore, we consider the religion of Aten in depth, we can at the most see in it a 'materialistic monotheism', if such a definition is not in itself absurd. It was not, therefore, spiritual, however great a degree of lyricism the poetical accents of the epileptic king might achieve, great enough to cause them to be mistaken for 'spirituality'. His famous 'Hymn', which has been compared with the *laudi* of St. Francis and undoubtedly has a close affinity with the 114th Psalm of David, is really a canticle addressed to the 'sun'—the physical entity presiding over physical life—without any preoccupation with eschatological problems.

The seed sown by Queen Tiy germinated quickly, favoured by the peculiar physico-psychological circumstances of Amenophis IV. The persecution of the priests of Amun gradually became more severe: the first measures, of a fiscal nature involving the reduction of the temple fees, were followed by the interdiction of the cult, the closing of the temples, and the elimination of the name of the Theban god. It would seem that the real persecution began in the fourth year of the king's reign: the Theban necropolis was meticulously inspected by agents sent there for that purpose, and wherever they found the name of the abhorred god, they obliterated it. Not even the statue of the king's father, Amenophis III, was respected, and from it, too, the name of the god was erased. The capital, however, which had previously been a centre of intense religious life, once the temples had been closed and the priesthood disbanded, at all events officially, must have exercised a depressing effect on the sovereign, who, moreover, did not feel too safe there. He could not possibly expect to receive the support of the masses; the populace, attached to the old traditions, could not accept, from one day to another, a new creed so far removed from the religious ideas hitherto professed. And the priests of Amun, defeated but not destroyed, were themselves waiting for a favourable opportunity to get rid of the king. All these considerations, as well as the general atmosphere of tension, must have weighed heavily on the mind of Amenophis IV, encouraging him to seek out a suitable site for the founding of a new city—a city without a past, free from the shadows of irate divinities, and dedicated solely to the cult of the new god, the physical sun, which would illuminate the sovereign and the faithful with its beneficent rays resembling outstretched arms. This new city would become the residence of his followers, forming a community of their own. There thus arose *Akhetaten* = the 'Horizon of Aten', on a pleasant bend of the Nile, half-way between the modern Cairo and Luxor. The ruins of this city, now known as Tell el-Amarna, have been excavated in particular by the 'Egypt

123

Exploration Society' and are of great interest, since they constitute one of the few Egyptian cities that have survived to the present day.

Even the king's name, Amenophis, could not be reconciled with the new religion and he changed it to Akhenaten = 'Aten is satisfied'.

Two other cities dedicated to Aten were built in other parts of the empire, in Nubia and in Asia; the site of the Asiatic city is unknown, but the ruins of the Nubian city have been identified near the modern Dulgo.

Politically, the young sovereign, obsessed by his prophetical spirit, proved himself to be quite inept, losing valuable allies and antagonizing powerful enemies. For this reason, State documents were addressed to the Queen Mother Tiy, as is proved by the letters written by Tushratta, king of Mitanni.

Akhenaten did not undertake any military campaigns, but he insisted on being represented with the 'blue crown', the equivalent of a military helmet, perhaps because he wanted to show in this way that he was in a perpetual state of conflict.

Together with his family—his wife Nefertiti and his daughters, the latter markedly hydrocephalic— Akhenaten moved to the new capital, and Thebes experienced its maximum period of decadence and desolation.

The impulse given to the arts by the king, 'the one and only prophet of Aten', was characterized by the direct instructions he gave to artists: peremptory orders which were obsequiously executed, while the artists took pains to emphasize that 'His Majesty' had taught them their art. Everything was conceived as having a direct anti-traditional function—a gigantic task of philosophical and aesthetical destruction, particularly violent during the first years of the reign. From that period, in fact, date the colossal statues of the king, tragic caricatures which show up his physical defects and in which, moreover, his Asiatic descent is clearly discernible (Plate 68). The king proclaimed that he wished to impose the *Mā'et* (='truth') at all costs, but it was a parody of truth rather than a faithful rendering of reality. Akhenaten's ideas and actions were all intended to be in direct opposition to the traditional Egyptian conceptions. The idea of the sacredness of royalty was destroyed by secularizing even the least important acts in the private lives of the sovereign and his family: domestic scenes (Plate 69), embracings in public, distribution of food, of which even his little daughters received their share and were depicted in the act of eating it—all these things were prescribed as 'models' for the artists, who had to draw their inspiration from plaster casts of the faces of the royal family. Defects were not allowed to be concealed; in fact they were, if possible, accentuated, from the deformed belly of Akhenaten to the hydrocephalic princesses and the ophthalmia of Nefertiti. There would seem to have been a passionate fury against all that which had hitherto been considered right, aesthetically correct and venerable: a sadistic pleasure in holding up to ridicule all that royalty had signified. But Akhenaten also had another characteristic—his pronounced egotism. The limelight of the artistic stage was concentrated on him and his family, and as the iconoclastic trend of the religion of Aten also prohibited images of the gods, except that of the solar disc with the rays emanating from it, the latter was the only one to be represented, but always in the act of blessing the royal family (Plate 70). Thus the tombs and chapels which private individuals erected in their own gardens were adorned with royal portraits, while private statues became rare exceptions. Akhenaten seems to have monopolized for himself and his family all the artists' ateliers in Amarna. C. Boreux, the Conservator of the Louvre, on the basis of the items preserved in the museum, thinks it quite probable that Akhenaten's religious reform compelled the Egyptians to replace the worship of divinities by that of the royal triad consisting of the king, his wife and his elder daughter.

The new religion, drawing its inspiration from Nature, ignored the world to come and consequently the tombs no longer contained representations of 'typical acts', but were transformed into mausoleums describing the owner's life, with exaltation of the figure of the king whenever possible: tombs, moreover, became a special privilege granted by the sovereign to his favourites. As regards Akhenaten himself, the subject of death was very rarely introduced. One scene shows him and his wife before the bier of his little daughter after her death, and the instructions given by the sovereign in the 'Dedicatory Inscription' include the following statement: 'A tomb shall be hewn for me in the eastern rocks and that shall be my sepulchre. . . . There shall be buried the Great Wife of the King, Nefertiti, and his daughter

Meritaten.' But it makes no reference to any doctrine of the other world; the classical sacramental formula of the 'king who flies to Heaven' is here replaced by instructions for interment. The king, incidentally, did not build a funerary temple.

In the tombs of the early period, to the south of the landing-place, the construction of which was discontinued about the eighth year of the reign, the royal family were regularly shown worshipping the sun, while in the tombs to the north the figures of the owners reappear. Certain memories of Thebes can be seen in the tomb of Huy, the superintendent of the royal harem.

The deceased, who under the Old Kingdom had been shown as a 'non-active' spectator, disappears from the scenes depicted in tombs, and narrative assumes the foremost place, with the owner shown 'in action' in events that had really taken place. For the first time the arrangement in horizontal rows is discarded so that the superimposed figures form part of one and the same scene. Nevertheless, the Amarna revolution, though it broke with most of the classical rules, did not succeed in changing the fundamental method of projecting human figures, which remained essentially 'frontal'.

Akhenaten soon had to realize the impossibility of imposing a new creed simply by proselytizing, since it was a question of achieving an essential change of conceptions and feeling. He had to fetter his followers with bonds of gold.

'Hang gold on his neck in front and behind and on his legs, for he has heard the teaching of the Pharaoh in all things.' That was what the king ordered should be done to Merirē', while the priest Ay declared: 'He [the king] redoubles the favours in gold and silver that he grants me,' and the army general Mai informs us: 'He has doubled his favours like grains of sand: I am the chief of the officers at the head of the people. My Lord has promoted me, because I have propagated his teachings and at every hour I listen to his words.'

And the sovereign, together with Nefertiti and his little daughter, is shown throwing collars of gold from the balcony of his palace.

But gold is a dangerous and unreliable chain. When Akhenaten fell, none of his partisans or followers were ready to fight for Aten. The tomb of Haremhab, who later ascended the throne, is an interesting example. Begun during the reign of Akhenaten, it shows all the influence of the doctrine of the moment. The building of it was interrupted on the death of the sovereign and later resumed, returning in every sense to the pre-Amarna schemes.

The first period, which we may describe as one of destruction and the introduction of new ideas, was followed by a more moderate phase, during which portraiture achieved a very high standard, sometimes quite unsurpassed (Plates 71, 72). Schaefer stresses the originality of Amarna artists, but is contradicted by Frankfort. The names of many artists of the period are known to us, among them the sculptor Tuthmosis, Iuty, the 'master artist of Queen Tiy', and Bek, 'trained by His Majesty'.

In painting, in addition to royal portraits, subjects

PLATE 52. Ritual dance, in the tomb of Kheruef at Thebes. Eighteenth Dynasty.

PLATE 53. Detail of a funeral dance. Fragment from a tomb in Sakkâra. Nineteenth Dynasty. Height of original 15¾ inches; 40 cm. *Cairo, Museum.*

PLATE 54. The "Geese of Meidûm". Polychrome fresco. Fourth Dynasty.
Cairo, Museum.

PLATE 55. Birds. Tomb of Nefer-her-Ptah in Sakkâra. Fifth Dynasty.

PLATE 56. Wrestlers. In a tomb at Beni-Hasan. Twelfth Dynasty.

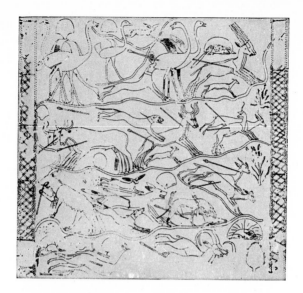

PLATE 57. Hunting in the desert showing "flying beasts". Tomb of the Vizier Rekhmere'. Eighteenth Dynasty. Graphical reconstruction. (*Cf. Bibliography under Groenewegen-Frankfort.*)

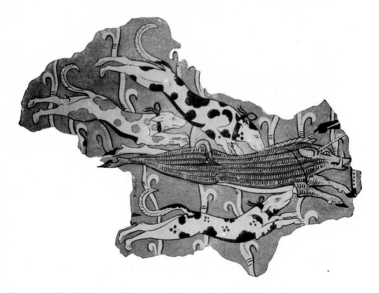

PLATE 58. Hunting scene. Fragment of a mural painting from the palace at Tiryns.

PLATE 59. Musicians and dancing-girls. Fragment of a painting from a Theban tomb of the Eighteenth Dynasty. *London, British Museum.*

PLATE 60. The dying fox. In the tomb of Userhat at Thebes. Eighteenth Dynasty.

PLATE 61. Agricultural scenes. In the tomb of Menna at Thebes.
Eighteenth Dynasty.

PLATE 62. Hunting with the boomerang. Fragment from a Theban tomb.
Reign of Sethos I, Nineteenth Dynasty. *London, British Museum.*

PLATE 63. Maidservant attending a lady. Fragment stolen from the tomb of Djeserkaraseneb at Thebes and later recovered. Eighteenth Dynasty.

PLATE 64. Agricultural scene. From the tomb of Sennedjem at Deir el-Medinêh.
Twentieth Dynasty.

PLATE 65. Detail from a satirical papyrus. Nineteenth Dynasty. *Cairo, Museum.*

Plate 66. *Ostracon* from Deir el-Medîneh, showing a girl swimming.
New Kingdom. *Turin, Museum.*

PLATE 67. Detail of a painted limestone statuette showing Akhenaten with an offertory tablet. Height 15¾ inches; 40 cm. *Cairo, Museum.*

PLATE 68. Detail of a colossal statue of Akhenaten in painted sandstone. From Karnak. Height of a similar whole statue 13 feet; 4 metres. *Cairo, Museum.*

PLATE 69. Unfinished group in limestone, showing Akhenaten and his daughter. From the workshop of the sculptor Tuthmosis at Tell el-Amarna. Height of original 16½ inches; 42 cm. *Cairo, Museum.*

drawn from Nature are represented—birds and other animals at liberty among papyri and bushes—while for the first time we can detect an attempt to break up the 'chromatic mono-tonality' by giving nuances to the colours.

As a result of the elimination of solemn poses, the human figure is rendered in freer attitudes, sometimes almost decadent in their relaxation. To a certain extent these attitudes influenced the period immediately following, especially the reign of Tutankhaten (Plate 84), who soon changed his name to Tutankhamun, thus confirming the complete re-establishment of the Theban god.

Akhenaten died shortly after 1350 B.C., unmourned by the populace who had not understood him and had remained secretly attached to the national traditions. Certainly the forces he represented were not constructive as regards the future of Egypt. In the arts the lack of any feeling for moderation, and excesses committed by the king's order, prevented the consolidation of those trends which, especially in portraiture, had achieved the highest possible standards. But the burden of the grotesque and of caricature, the parodying of sacred things and the 'veristic' exaltation of negative aspects, involved these tendencies too in the collapse of Amarna. And perhaps the gravest fault of Akhenaten was that he could not discern the enormous possibilities which, despite the destruction of traditional canons and the reaction towards an anti-natural grotesqueness, might have been realized by certain exceptional artists. It would have been necessary to separate these pure manifestations of art from the exaggerations created by the desire to destroy tradition; left to themselves, they might have survived, but, united, they had to pay the price of such an association. This, however, would mean expecting too much from Akhenaten, who may have been a true prophet, but was certainly a bad Pharaoh.

CHAPTER EIGHT

Architecture

To DEAL with the whole of Egyptian architecture within the limits of one chapter, almost incidentally, would be an absurd undertaking if we did not pre-suppose a necessary restriction to its fundamental aspects, and above all to its artistic, rather than its technical, side.

The monumental ruins, often grandiose, majestic-ally isolated in the midst of the desert or bottled up among the traffic of the cities, contribute towards an idea of ancient Egyptian architecture which is not quite correct.

Whatever their state of preservation, great stone edifices present themselves to our gaze almost as evidence of a continual aspiration towards the 'masto-dontic'—temples built to glorify the various divinities or funerary edifices erected to glorify sovereigns. The desire to 'exalt' which inspired their construction led the old architects to vie with one another in their search for forms as majestic as possible, worthy of those whom they were intended to honour.

But temples and mausoleums cannot, and in fact do not, represent a people's only forms of architectural expression, and if we limit our study to relics of this kind we can easily fall into an error.

It is true that of the cities of the living very little remains, for wood and clay, the raw materials used in the construction of houses, have long since crumbled into dust. The surviving walls of Akhenaten's city enable us to make only partial reconstructions, which are nevertheless interesting, and the same may be said of the other towns brought to light by archaeological excavations; but the further we return towards the early historical periods the more the elements become impalpable, until they finally disappear altogether, and are replaced by more or less theoretical reconstructions. Let us, nevertheless, starting from the examples that have come down to us, endeavour to trace an outline of the history of Egyptian architecture.

Speaking generally, architecture can be divided into the following categories:

Civil architecture (cities); funerary architecture (necropolises); religious architecture (temples, religious buildings, etc.); and military architecture. Each of these comprises elements peculiar to that one category and elements which may be common to two or more.

Logically enough, of the oldest prehistoric period we possess neither relics nor memories of the dwellings of the living, but it is not difficult to imagine what kind of habitations the primitive inhabitants of the Nile Valley must have had. In the earliest times Upper Egypt was the home of nomad hunters, who probably dwelt in light and easily portable tents, to protect themselves in particular from the heat, since in those days the climate was semi-tropical. After the introduction of agriculture, and the consequent establishment of permanent settlements, the first villages began to form—groups of huts made of clay mixed with straw, supported by palm-branches and leaves, enclosed within a palisade. The identification of the objects painted on vases from Abydos is still a matter of dispute: some scholars maintain that they are prehistoric villages, others that they are boats.

Nevertheless, we know the types of chapels or 'sanctuaries' that were built during this early epoch—places dedicated to the worship of a local god. These primitive religious edifices, known as *Iteret*, vary according to whether they are in Upper or Lower Egypt. In the former case they seem to have been

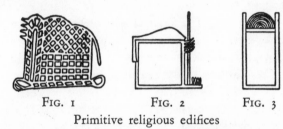

FIG. 1   FIG. 2   FIG. 3

Primitive religious edifices

edifices with a wooden framework covered by a skin, perhaps deriving from the primitive tents of the nomad chiefs. The outlines were like those of a large animal, an elephant or rhinoceros, with tusks in front, humped backs and tails. Sometimes they looked as if they were resting on sledges, which would be a confirmation of their origins in the nomadic period, when the necessity of frequent changes of location would favour the use of a light *naos* that could be easily dragged over the sand. For that matter, even during the historical period various religious symbols —boats, *naos*, catafalques, etc.—were often drawn over the sand on sledges. In later times the form of these shrines was stylized to such an extent that they lost the features which had characterized them in early days: the back of the symbolical animal assumes the shape of a roof, while the tail seems to have become a hanging curtain; the claws become horizontal bars and two pinnacles were erected on either side of the doorway and remained down to historical times to mark the entrance and supports for draperies and festoons (Figs. 1, 2, 3).

In Lower Egypt, where the first agricultural populations settled, the 'temple' had a more permanent character, with a vaulted roof and, presumably, walls of crude bricks. The vault as an architectural element appeared in the remotest times and the granaries of baked earth found during the excavations at Helwan by Zaki Saad have the cupola shape well known to the potters of those days, on the brink between the early historic and the prehistoric periods. When we remember that clay was the raw material of the buildings themselves, we realize that buildings of this sort must have been influenced by those craftsmen who were most familiar with clay (Fig. 3). To sum up, pre-dynastic architecture was influenced by two phases in the lives of the primitive inhabitants—nomadic and settled—and developed in accordance with both these aspects, without leaving any visible traces that can be described as 'monumental'. With the advent of the historical period traces of this kind begin to appear and we now find tombs of kings, officials and private individuals, and also silos, like those found by Gilbert at el-Kab.

The material used for such buildings was still crude

brick, but the excavations at Helwan already mentioned show that squared blocks of limestone were being used as early as the First Dynasty. This discovery has modified the earlier theories, which attributed to the reign of Zoser (Third Dynasty) the first use of stone in architecture. The new classification of tombs made by Reisner is now generally accepted; he divided funerary edifices into five categories, which we will now briefly examine.

Type I. Shaft tombs built of crude bricks and covered with wooden roofs. Among the royal tombs of this type we may mention that assigned by Petrie and Reisner to Menes, who unified Egypt and founded the First Dynasty. The fact that in this tomb the ivory tablet of King Hor-Aha, 'the fighter', was found, led to the identification of Menes with Hor-Aha. Of the same type is the tomb of Narmer, which also consists of a single chamber. Those of Djer and Djer-Uadji consist of a large chamber lined with wood, divided into compartments and surrounded by store-rooms. Private tombs of this type have been found at Abydos, Gizeh and at Tarkhan.

Type II. Similar to the preceding, but with the addition of a staircase giving access to it. To this type belong the First Dynasty royal tombs of Udimu, Adjib, Semerkhet and Ka-a. That of the last-named is partially vaulted.

Type III. Vaulted tombs to which access was gained by means of a staircase, e.g. the royal tombs of Peribsen and Khasekhem dating from the Second Dynasty.

Type IV. Consisting of several compartments to which access was gained by means of a long staircase.

To this category we can assign, with certain reservations, the layer pyramid of Zawiyet-el-Aryan and the Second and Third Dynasty private tombs at Memphis.

Type V. Access to these is gained by means of a sloping corridor hewn in the rock, while the burial chamber is of brick and at the bottom of an open shaft. To this category belong the tombs of Zoser (Third Dynasty), the unfinished pyramid of Zawiyet-el-Aryan (not to be confused with that mentioned above), and the pyramids at Mēdūm and Dahshûr. Mention should also be made of the tomb at Negadah discovered by De Morgan, who attributed it to Menes, whereas the tendency nowadays is to connect it with the name of Queen Neithotep of the First Dynasty. This tomb is important because part of the superstructure has been preserved, which is not the case with the tombs at Abydos. Here we have the type of tomb known as *mastabas*, from the Arabic word meaning 'bench', owing to the resemblance between such edifices and the benches of beaten clay found in modern villages. This tomb, like that of Hor-Aha, has on its façade a series of grooves which give animation to the wall and, with the interplay of light and shade, break the monotony. The walls are of crude bricks cased, externally, with plaster, which was generally painted in bright colours with ornamental geometric motives. In the course of Emery's recent excavations at Sakkâra, which brought to light the tomb of Queen Herneith of the First Dynasty, the author of the present volume was able to detect many traces of the original colouring—the pavement of mud bricks coloured white, a green corridor, lateral niches in yellow above a first coating of white 'priming', and a central niche coloured red.

These niches, or grooves, have given rise to a number of hypotheses: an imitation of the façade of a royal palace, the reproduction of a walled structure which also had a 'magical' purpose, such as is likewise found on Old Kingdom sarcophagi. This last hypothesis, however, seems inadmissible, since a defensive enclosure with so many 'entrance gates' would have been, to say the least, absurd. Far more probable is Reisner's suggestion that these niches may have been the prototypes of the 'false doors', the object of which was to allow the deceased's *Ka* to emerge during the daylight hours and enjoy the funerary offerings. This hypothesis finds confirmation in the famous Third Dynasty *mastaba* of Hesirēʿ, where these niches form an internal corridor and each of them is fitted with a wooden shutter, with the figure of the owner executed on it in a fairly advanced technique, which we have already had occasion to mention elsewhere in this volume.

The origin of the *mastaba* as an architectural type probably goes back to the 'tumulus' or mound of earth which covered the burial-place. Typical examples of this primitive type have been found at Naga ed-Deir, where the graves are covered with little heaps of stones and clay forming a compact mass. Nevertheless, bricks were already coming into use at that time, and one can detect the first attempts to execute the grooves and niches on the wall which we have mentioned above.

The *mastaba* was thus an intermediate stage between

the tumulus and the pyramid, and at the beginning,
as we have seen, was a simple rectangular superstructure round a central shaft, easy of access, which
constituted the burial chamber. Round the edifice ran
a wall, the height of which was limited so that it
would not obstruct the view of the ornamental
façade, and this wall formed a corridor along all four
sides. Access was gained to it through a gateway in
the eastern wall, and the funerary offerings were
placed in front of the central niches on this side. In
the already-mentioned tomb of Queen Herneith
the central niche was flanked by two bulls' heads
made of clay, with real horns. A similar example had
already been discovered by Emery at Sakkâra, where
a *mastaba* of exceptional size (215 × 125 feet), attributed to the third king of the First Dynasty, Uadji,
had a brick shelf running round the superstructure,
on which similar bulls' heads were placed. It may be
that here, and also in the case of Herneith's tomb,
such heads were placed all round the superstructure,
but only two have been found, flanking the central
niche on the east. The tomb of King Uadji was
surrounded by sixty-two graves outside the enclosure wall, containing the bodies of the servants and
courtiers who were destined to accompany their
master to the netherworld. This brings up once again
the question of human sacrifices, of which the early
dynastic period would seem to offer the last traces in
Egypt proper, but this is a theme which would lead
us too far away from our subject. It will be sufficient
if we mention that this custom was revived during the
Middle Kingdom, among the Cushite peoples of

Kerma, and later (down to the second century B.C.) at Meroë. This would show clearly that such a practice was due to the African substratum of the Nilotic peoples, and that it was abandoned when the increasing expansion of agriculture gradually brought about inevitable psychological changes and a trend towards ethically superior forms of civilization, though it persisted in areas where the African substratum still asserted itself vigorously.

The primitive type of *mastaba* soon proved quite inadequate for the protection of the deceased against the robbers of tombs, who were evidently active from the earliest times in the areas used as necropolises. It was thus necessary to resort to systems of defence which influenced the architectural evolution of such edifices. The store-rooms surrounding the central shaft leading to the burial chamber were filled in, so that the body of the edifice became a compact mass. From the roof shafts were sunk which, after traversing the edifice vertically, were driven several yards (20 or 30) into the solid rock. At the bottom of these shafts, and at right-angles to them, the various sepulchral chambers were excavated, into which the sarcophagus and the deceased's chattels were lowered. Lastly the shafts themselves were filled from above with blocks intended to prevent any attempt at violation. A vain hope, for almost all the tombs that have come down to us were violated in very early times. The burial chamber was located vertically beneath the 'chapel', which thus became an interior compartment, or more exactly underneath the 'false door' in front of which were placed the funerary offerings. The already-mentioned tomb of Hesirē, shows the evolution of the niches as false doors and the novelty of the inside chapel. The form of the latter assumed various shapes, 'cruciform', 'palace façade', etc., but these details have no specific importance as regards our study. The body of the *mastaba* continued to be in mud brick, especially at Gizeh, but stone was the principle material from the Fourth Dynasty onwards (Fig. 4).

What matters for the purposes of our study is the external appearance of such edifices, which characterized funerary architecture during the early historical period. Useful information can, moreover, be gleaned from them, because it is evident that there must have been some connexion, even if it were not as definite as some scholars suppose, between architectural and decorative forms and the dwellings of the living at the same time. The coloured tapestries with elaborate patterns reproduced both on the external façades and on the inner walls, the objects represented in the tomb of Hesirē', are all elements which help to give us a clearer idea of the state of Egyptian civilization during the somewhat obscure period in which those tendencies matured that, combined to form schemes, characterized the historical period.

From the primitive tumulus covering the remains of the deceased was derived, as we have said, the *mastaba*, the size of which was in direct proportion to the importance of the owner. During the Third Dynasty, thanks to the genius of that great architect Imhotep, the *mastabas* assumed a new architectural rôle and helped to inscribe a decisive page in the history of building. In the first place the mud bricks were replaced by limestone: a perishable material was replaced by durable stone, which might have defied eternity had it not been for that most destructive element of all—the vandalistic hands of men. Imhotep's innovations were not, however, confined

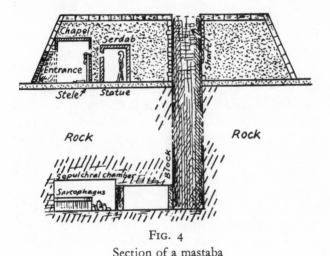

FIG. 4
Section of a mastaba

to the choice of materials, since for that matter, as we have already seen, limestone was already in use at Helwan during the First Dynasty. But Imhotep also evolved a grandiose new artistic conception. The original plan included an elaborate complex of religious edifices, all of stone, built round a great *mastaba* in honour of his sovereign, King Zoser.

The original *mastaba* had a square base, unique of

its kind, with sides measuring 206 feet, and was 25 feet high, but this initial project underwent a series of modifications which gradually altered its character, and it was transformed into a number of *mastabas*, superimposed and diminishing in size, in other words into a 'stepped' pyramid. After completion the edifice consisted of six 'steps', with a total height of 192 feet and sides measuring respectively 355 and 400 feet. The casing was of blocks of white limestone from Tura, which gave a homogeneous aspect to the whole. That the realization of the pyramid was the result of successive modifications of the original plan is of little importance for the purposes of our study, nor is it necessary for us to examine in detail the various sepulchral chambers inside it. We have, however, reproduced (Plate 4) the portrait of the king on one of the subterranean stelae and we may make a brief mention of the 'blue rooms', i.e. rooms lined with faïence tiles applied to the walls in a network pattern and on the door, forming an interesting decoration based on symbols of Osiris.

The pyramid stands in the midst of an architectural complex of notable elegance, enclosed within a perimeter wall and forming a rectangle about one square mile in extent (Fig. 5). The perimeter wall provides clear evidence of the transition from mud bricks to blocks of stone, for the shape of the bricks is retained by way of convention, including the holes originally intended for the insertion of the vegetable fibre which bound them together. The height of this wall was originally about $34\frac{1}{2}$ feet and the recesses executed on it can be related to the similar niches in the mud-brick *mastabas*. The main structure and all its component parts remain as if petrified. There would seem to have been only one entrance, on the east side, consisting of a narrow corridor flanked on either side by twenty columns and leading to a hall the ceiling of

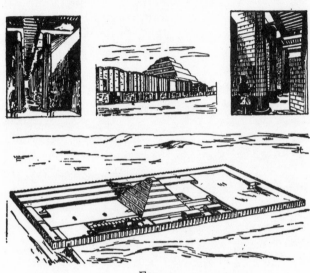

FIG. 5
The monumental complex of King Zoser
(Third Dynasty) at Sakkâra

which is borne by eight more columns. From the entrance corridor access was gained to the *Sed* court. At either end of the colonnade, that is to say at the entrance and at the exit, which is through the above-mentioned hall, two imitation doors were constructed as if they were open, so as to allow freedom of movement to the Pharaoh's *Ka*.

This would confirm the hypothesis we have already advanced concerning the niches of the *mastabas*, which had in fact some connexion with the false doors.

The columns of the entrance corridor are not free-standing, but carved semicircular blocks emerging from the wall, so as to form a series of niches. The short walls connecting them do not strike the eye, since they are progressively masked by the succession of columns, and when we stand at the beginning of the colonnade and look down it, it seems as if we were looking at circular free-standing columns. The columns are of the 'fluted' type, but with the peculiarity that the fluting is convex instead of concave. According to Lauer, they were originally painted red. The upper portions look as if they were fasciculated and only at three points is the fluting carried along the main axes. The ceiling reproduces in stone the semicircular wooden beams of the buildings of that time, while light was admitted through lateral openings. Of the other religious edifices built round the pyramid, few traces have remained, but these are sufficient to indicate a generally sober trend, and at the same time a refined taste, especially in the attention paid to details. The *Sed* court, where the sovereign held periodical jubilees, had forty-two shrines in which the statues of the divine representatives of the *nomes* of Egypt were accommodated when they attended the ceremony. Of great importance were the two houses of the North and South, interesting especially on account of their decorations, among these a papyriform column with a special kind of capital. And while we are dealing with the subject, it will be as well to give a summary description of the various types of columns used in Egyptian architecture.

First of all, we must explain the fundamental difference between the Egyptian and the Greek column, since our modern aesthetic ideas are under the direct influence of the latter. In Greece the column was the 'aesthetic expression of the balance of the human body', whereas in Egypt it was a realistic

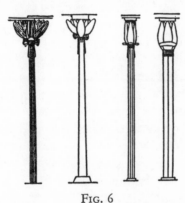

Fig. 6

Types of lotus-shaped column

representation of the stem and flower of a plant. Obviously the origin of the column conceived as a support must have been a tree-trunk stripped of its leaves and masked—very probably—with bunches of flowers. Such may well have been the origin of the most typical Egyptian column—the 'floral' column with its basic types: 'lotus-shaped', 'papyrus-shaped' and 'palm-shaped'.

The lotus-bud column is represented by three

varieties of this plant: the *Nymphaea lotus* or white lotus; the *Nymphaea caerulea* or blue lotus; and at a later period the *Nelumbium speciosum* or pink lotus. All three varieties are represented with buds either open or closed (Fig. 6). The lotus column disappeared after the Middle Kingdom, but made its reappearance in a composite form during the Ptolemaic era.

The papyrus column used the varieties *Cyperus papyrus* and *Papyrus alopecuroides*, with both open and closed buds as in the preceding case. Combined in several stems, generally eight, it became the 'clustered' column. Two stylistic variants of this type can be seen in the Fifth Dynasty tomb of Niuserrē'; one angular and hard, but slender; the other softened and made heavier by rounded lines. Of these two types, only the latter survived after the New Kingdom. Clustered papyriform columns with open flowers are to be seen in the palace of Akhenaten, and, generally speaking, this type was used to support the central beams of hypostyle halls (Fig. 7).

The palmiform type reproduces the *Phoenix dactylifera*, i.e. the date-palm, and is one of the oldest forms, already in use in the days of Sahurē' (Fifth Dynasty) and consisting of a stylized form of the actual tree (Fig. 8). During the Late Period we even find the fallen leaves represented at the bottom of the stem.

With the advent of the New Kingdom and the spread of Baroque taste, 'composite' floral capitals were created by amalgamating and superimposing different types of plants, with buds either open or closed.

Apart from the floral capital, there existed a particular type called the Hathor column, which was a representation of the sistrum, the musical instrument sacred to the Goddess of Love. The shaft supported a representation of the goddess's head, surmounted by a special shrine. Typical examples of such columns are to be found at Deir el-Bahri and Dendera.

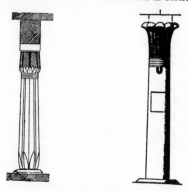

Fig. 7a. and b.
The papyrus-shaped (a) and palm-shaped (b) types of column

As a decoration for the 'Houses of the North and South', and also for the chapels used during the *Heb-Sed* festival forming part of the Zoser complex, we find a capital unique in the history of Egyptian art, consisting of two pointed leaves hanging laterally on the fluted shaft. This type puzzled scholars for a long time, as regards its identification with any vegetable species of ancient Egypt, and Lauer himself admitted that he had been unable to discover what the plant was. P. E. Newberry finally identified it as a variety, now extinct in Egypt, of the *Heracleum giganteum* and supported his assertion by means of experiments made with a specimen of the plant, which he himself cultivated. This particular kind of plant also seems to have influenced the 'little models' of columns found by Petrie in the tombs of Udimu and Djer at Abydos, and by Firth at Sakkâra in a *mastaba* of Udimu's time, as well as the form of some vases found in the subterranean chambers of King Zoser's step pyramid.

To return to the evolution of the superstructure of tombs, from the tumulus and the *mastaba* to the pyramid, we must here draw attention to a philological factor of some importance. In the 'Pyramid Texts', one of the oldest designations for 'tomb' is *Ia*, and the sign denoting it is either a truncated pyramid, almost a *mastaba*, or a pyramid complete with point. Between the stepped *mastaba* of Zoser and the pyramid of Cheops at Gizeh, however, lie several phases of evolution. The 'buried' pyramid of King Sekhemkhet, discovered by Zakaria Goneim at Sakkâra, presumably consisted of seven steps, and the two pyramids of Zawiyet-el-Aryan, a few miles south of Gizeh, must also have been stepped pyramids, though both of them are now in a sadly deteriorated state.

Of the three pyramids attributed to Snefru, the first king of the Fourth Dynasty, that at Mēdūm is chronologically the earliest. The layout of buildings forming it was to remain the classical model: a reception temple in the valley, facing the zone flooded by the Nile, and a 'sacred' causeway connecting with another temple at a higher level, the funerary temple, which backed on to the pyramid.

From the architectural point of view the best

known of Snefru's pyramids is the one described as being 'rhomboidal' because of the twofold inclination of the walls. These, in fact, start from the base at an angle of 54° 14′, which diminishes to 42° 59′ towards the top. According to Varille this inclination was intentional and had a symbolical meaning. This is contrary to the opinion of other scholars, among them Perring, who think that it is a matter of pure chance. The pyramid in question is 318 feet 10 inches high with sides measuring 618 feet 9 inches. A peculiar feature is that it has two separate entrances, leading into chambers at different levels.

The third pyramid of Snefru is called the 'Northern Pyramid' of Dahshûr and represents the stage nearest to the perfectly geometrical form of the true pyramid. Its inclination is very slight, and as the limestone casing that originally covered the outside has now disappeared, it displays the inner masonry, which is of a reddish colour.

It was left to Cheops, the son and successor of Snefru, to erect that stone monument which in the days of Antiquity was ranked as one of the Seven Wonders of the World—the Great Pyramid at Gizeh.

The traditions and legends connected with this monument are known the world over, from the narrative of Herodotus to the chronicles of the various travellers who have described it in the course of the centuries. Modern historical criticism, however, has demolished the reputation of a slave-driver and a cruel tyrant attributed to Cheops, and has shown how, on the contrary, he solved the problem of unemployment during the Inundation period. His name was not execrated, but was considered to have magic virtues, and it was inscribed on many scarab-amulets of a later epoch.

The monument rises to a height of 479 feet on a square base each side of which is 754 feet long, and according to an approximate calculation consists of two million three hundred thousand blocks of limestone from the local quarries, discovered in comparatively recent times (Fig. 9). The fine quality of limestone used for the outer casing, of which only traces remain, came on the other hand from Tura. The inclination of the walls from the horizontal is 51° 52', and it is interesting to note the accurate siting of the walls of the pyramid with regard to the cardinal points. This is a reflexion of certain religious beliefs, since at that time the doctrine relating to the paradise of the Pharaohs had a definitely 'stellar' character: the king, as we learn from the 'Pyramid Texts', 'rises' (from his pyramid) to the heaven amidst the Imperishable Stars (i.e. those around the Poles). It was not until the Fifth Dynasty that the 'solar' doctrine began to prevail, but before that time the orientation of the pyramids in relation to the circumpolar stars was of the highest importance. A curious detail is furnished by the *Sebaites*, members of a sect of star-worshippers. If we remember that in old Egyptian *seba* means 'star', the connexion between the huge stone monument and the cult of the stars becomes clearer. The orientation of the sides of the edifice was presumably done by the sovereign himself, considering the invariable rôle played by the kings of Egypt in the ceremonies connected with the foundation of temples. Instruments have come down to us which were also used in later times to determine the orientation of temples: the *merkhet*, literally 'palm keel of the watcher of the hours', in other words the plumb-line, together with the texts engraved on the instrument to explain how

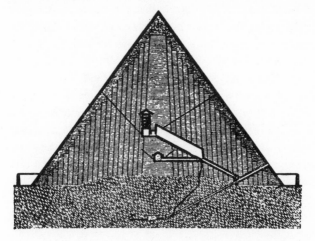

FIG. 8

Section of the Great Pyramid of Cheops at Gizeh
(after Borchardt)

to use it: 'I take the level and grasp the handle of the mallet with Seshat [the goddess of calculation]. I have turned my gaze in accordance with the movement of the stars and directed it towards the constellation of the Great Bear . . . I have established the four corners of thy temple.' Regarding the king's share in the function, we read that he was 'the image of Ishedes [a name given to the god Thoth, patron of the exact sciences], skilful in the use of the *merkhet*'.

Very little has remained of the funerary edifices dedicated to the cult of Cheops, since the area has been ravaged several times in history in the course of the search for stone. The remains of the valley temple lie beneath the modern Arab village; nothing remains of the 'sacred way', but the investigations made by Abu-Seif and Lauer have yielded a certain number of details concerning the funerary temple erected in front of the east side of the pyramid. An important element in Egyptian architecture, which is already found in the oldest buildings, was the pillar, usually of granite, with a square or rectangular profile. It owes its origin to the desire to utilize as supports large blocks which had been more or less squared. The oldest examples bear no inscriptions, but later on they were adorned with hieroglyphs or even with scenes. They were also used in *mastabas*, e.g. in that of Ptahhotep at Sakkâra, with the name of the owner inscribed upon them. Sometimes a statue of the god Osiris, or of the king in the form of this god, was erected against the pillar, which in such cases is called an 'Osiride pillar'. Such statues, however, must not, from the technical point of view, be confused with the Greek caryatids, since the Egyptians never used statues as supports. Characteristic examples are the colossal statues of Ramesses II, here too in Osiride form, in the Ramesseum at Thebes.

The geometrical proportions of the Great Pyramid have given rise to many theories, some of them undoubtedly fantastic. The fact remains, however, that these proportions exist and help to make the monument in question a synthesis of the technical knowledge of those ancient craftsmen. The pure geometrical form has in itself an aesthetic value and in its concrete aspect crystallizes those laws of equilibrium and harmony to which the Egyptians tried to remain as far as possible faithful. When we stand at the foot of the monument its great bulk—as an entity of weight—disappears, and the eye, gliding along the inclined planes, induces the psychological idea of elevation, and, one might say, a sense of levitation.

In the scientific field the controversy still continues between the advocates of the theory according to which the great pyramids of the Gizeh group were painted, and those who deny this. Pochan, supported by the authority of the spectral analysis made at the Sorbonne of samples from the casing of the pyramid of Cheops, maintains that this pyramid was painted red. Lauer, relying on the analysis made by Dr. Zaki Iskandar of the Cairo Museum, definitely denies this, though he makes certain reservations in the case of the pyramid of Menkaurē'. For the purposes of a more complete aesthetic valuation it would certainly be interesting to have a reliable answer to this question, and it is to be hoped that future research will be able to give a definite decision.

The other two 'great' pyramids are respectively of smaller dimensions: that of Khafrē' (Chephren) originally had a height of 470 feet with sides 706 feet long; that of Menkaurē' (Mycerinus) was 204 feet high and with sides 356 feet long.

Of Chephren's religious edifices, the funerary temple, the best preserved of all the Gizeh group, has survived, together with the valley temple and remains of the 'sacred way' connecting the two. The valley temple has considerable importance for the study of ritual, for in it Grsdeloff identified the spot where the 'tent of purification' formerly stood, in which the body of the king was purified with holy water and then embalmed. The façade of the temple, facing east, had two entrances, each flanked by two sphinxes, leading into an antechamber with granite walls and alabaster pavement. From the antechamber a door gave access to the T-shaped hypostyle hall similar in shape to 'purification tanks', with which it may have had some ideal connexion. Here too the floor was of alabaster, while the ceiling was borne by sixteen monolithic pillars, square except for two which were rectangular. Light reached the interior through lateral apertures along the upper sides of the roof, which was immersed in semi-darkness. The interior, with its smooth and perfectly squared granite pilasters, and the translucent alabaster floor, formed a very sober and elegant ensemble: twenty-three statues in alabaster, slate and diorite, showing the sovereign seated on his throne, adorned the walls. We run no risk of exaggerating if we say that an edifice of this kind represented an aesthetic zenith in Old Kingdom temple architecture. The 'sacred way' began at the north-east corner of the hypostyle hall; 540 yards long and 15 feet wide, it terminated at the antechamber of the funerary hall. In all probability, like other 'sacred ways' of this type, it too was decorated internally with scenes from the sovereign's life. Hölscher maintains that the custom of decorating such 'ways' with scenes of this kind did not begin until the Fifth Dynasty, but this would appear to be contradicted by the discovery of blocks with carvings belonging to the 'sacred way' of Cheops.

As regards the actual funerary temple, during the Old Kingdom it had a rectangular ground-plan and consisted of a portion open to the public and of the 'sancta sanctorum' to which only the priests entrusted with the performance of the rites had access. Here, too, the raw materials were granite and alabaster. In hypothetical reconstructions of such an edifice some scholars have introduced two *serdabs*, or cells, for funerary statues, one for Upper and one for Lower Egypt. The courtyard is said to have been adorned with pillars and the latter, according to Hölscher, were of the Osiride type. This hypothesis is disputed by Ricke, and the presence of such statues would in fact have been strange at a time when the religion of Osiris was still confined to the lower strata of the populace. As a matter of fact, no statue of this kind has ever been found.

There is another monumental complex connected with Chephren that cannot be ignored—the great Sphinx and its temple.

Surrounded since the days of Antiquity by legends, to such an extent that the very word 'sphinx' has become a synonym for 'mystery', this monument has watched the rising of the sun for thousands of years, while the problem of the date of its origin and its real purpose has remained unsolved. Only comparatively recent archaeological excavations, in particular those directed by Professor Selim Hassan, have provided evidence in support of a tentative thesis, which is now generally accepted.

We have already said that the limestone used in the construction of the great pyramid of Cheops came from local quarries situated to the south-east of the pyramid itself. By the time the pyramid had been finished, nothing remained in the quarries but a virtually unusable mass of rock. When the valley temple of Chephren was built, the architects found themselves confronted by this mass and preferred to convert it into a monument rather than face the formidable task of demolishing it and levelling the ground. They thus created this mythical stone animal with the body of a lion and the forepaws stretching out to the front, and with a human face reproducing the features of the king. Originally it was completely covered by a layer of painted plaster, of which only a few ochre-coloured traces remain on the face, which has unfortunately been badly mutilated. The monument is 66 feet high and 187 feet long; to give an idea of its dimensions, the nose measures 5 feet 7 inches and the ear 4 feet 6 inches. The temple of the Sphinx lies in front of the huge animal, and seems to be identical, as regards its façade, with the neighbouring valley temple of Chephren, though the interior is quite different. A large courtyard measuring 140 by 75 feet was surrounded by rectangular pillars and open in the centre, so as to give a view of the Sphinx. The west wall of the outer perimeter was hewn out of the solid rock to a height of 8 feet 2 inches, while the upper portion was then made higher by placing huge blocks upon it. This still leaves us puzzled as to the technical methods employed, and we are even more puzzled when we study the whole complex of the Chephren edifices: in the temple vestibule there are blocks weighing 38, 42, and 150 tons, and others in the temple itself weighing 452 tons. So far as we know, these blocks were moved only with the aid of simple levers and men's arms. In this connexion we should remember that the colossus of Ramesses II, now in fragments in the courtyard of the Ramesseum, was 56 feet high and had a total weight of a thousand tons!

The little pyramids of the queens at Gizeh contribute nothing to our technical and artistic knowledge. The same may be said of the pyramid of Userkaf at Sakkâra. The Fifth Dynasty pyramids at Abusir follow the classical pattern: a reception temple in the valley, a 'sacred way', and a funerary temple beside the pyramid, but there are a number of structural variations in the temple buildings, to which dwellings for the priests were added. For us, that is to say from the point of view of aesthetical valuation, the Gizeh complex, in so far as the pyramids are concerned, constitutes the *non plus ultra*. All other edifices of this kind dating from later periods have a purely historical value and, for example in the case of the pyramid of Unis, a philological and religious value, since the walls of its funerary chambers have the famous 'Pyramid Texts' inscribed upon them. We must not, however, underestimate the great importance of the scenes reproduced along the 'sacred ways' of the various pyramids of the period; many of these came to light during the recent excavations at Sakkâra and several examples of them have already been mentioned.

As regards the evolution of temples during the Old Kingdom, we must emphasize the influence of the 'double' aspect of the Pharaonic monarchy, which synthesized the Kingdoms of Upper and Lower Egypt. The respect the Pharaoh had to show for the ritual customs peculiar to each of the two kingdoms, which differed in many points, has left its mark on architecture. Moreover, the rise and development of the solar doctrine, which was already beginning to make itself felt in Chephren's time, influenced building activity in the sense that it led to the erection of ante-temples, these being almost repetitions of the valley temples. Ricke and Schott stress the survival of the rites peculiar to each of the two kingdoms: in the Thinite era the sovereigns had two tombs, one at Abydos and the other at Sakkâra. The former had superstructures of the tumulus, and therefore primitive, type, while the latter had the form of houses. A detailed study of the influence of this dualistic conception, in all its architectural and ritual manifestations, would take us too far. It is sufficient for our purpose merely to mention its existence.

The funerary temples of the pyramids were in any case destined only for the cult of the sovereign. Monumental remains dating from the Fifth Dynasty bear witness to the construction of a solar temple by Niuserrē'. The importance of this edifice is due especially to the great four-sided obelisk erected on a monumental terrace. In reality this is a truncated pyramid serving as a base for the obelisk, with a casing of granite blocks at the bottom, while limestone is used for the upper portion. The obelisk was about 117 feet high, and, in contrast to the more recent type, was not a monolith, but built of limestone blocks

The obelisk was one of the most typical monuments of ancient Egypt. The Egyptian name for it was *tekhen*, the modern name being derived from the Greek word meaning 'spear', and ever since the remotest times it has been associated with sun-worship, almost as if it were a petrified ray of the divine star.

Obelisks of small size appear during the Old Kingdom in front of private tombs and also in front of the pyramid of Neith (reign of Pepy II), their height in the latter case being 4 feet 8 inches. At Tanis, what is probably a fragment from an obelisk has been found bearing the name of Chephren, as well as two others bearing the name of Pepy II. The obelisk was considered as being a divine entity and as such could receive the appropriate worship and offerings. For us, however, the ritual aspect is of less interest than the aesthetic form. From small obelisks we pass to the great monoliths of the New Kingdom, more than a hundred feet high, like that of Tuthmosis III and IV now at Rome in the square in front of St. John Lateran. The top, or 'pyramidion', which the Egyptians call *benbenet*, was often covered with gold leaf and this accentuated its character of solar splendour. In the early days obelisks were usually placed in pairs in front of temples and tombs, and this 'dualism' may be a result of the idea we have mentioned above. In the Aswân quarries one of these monoliths is still *in loco*, thus providing us with information as to the methods used in cutting the rock horizontally, while scenes in the temple at Deir el-Bahri show the boats used for transporting the obelisks from the quarries to the place of erection.

Obelisks can be either perfectly smooth or carved, usually with dedicatory inscriptions by the Pharaoh in honour of the divinity, while the 'pyramidion' is sometimes decorated with scenes showing the sovereign making offerings to the god. The holy city of obelisks was, even in Old Kingdom times, Heliopolis, the biblical On, where the local religion was markedly solar. There, during the Middle Kingdom, the Pharaoh Sesostris I had an engraved obelisk erected, 66 feet high, the base of which has quite recently come to light. It was the first really tapered monolithic obelisk with the characteristics that later became classical features under the New Kingdom. This was the period that witnessed the erection of the great obelisks at Thebes dedicated to Amun, for example those of Queen Hatshepsut, of the various Tuthmoses, and of Ramesses II now in Piazza del Popolo at Rome, of Ramesses II in front of the Pantheon, and the small one known as the 'Dogali' obelisk, down to the late obelisks of Psammetikos II at Monte Citorio and Apries in Piazza della Minerva.

The obelisk is in itself a complete monument. In its extreme simplicity and purity of line it achieves a compromise between soaring height and equilibrium, and is static and dynamic at the same time. The little pyramid formed by the apex projects itself skywards, accentuating the upward thrust of the monolith's already slightly inclined planes. As regards the obelisks in Rome, it is certainly to be deplored from the aesthetic point of view that an excess of religious zeal has shattered their harmony by suffocating the 'pyramidion' beneath the weight of hundreds of

PLATE 70. The solar disc of Aten blessing the royal family: Akhenaten, Nefertiti and their three daughters. Stele from Tell el-Amarna. *Cairo, Museum.*

PLATE 71. Unfinished quartzite head of Queen Nefertiti. Height of original 13 inches; 33 cm. *Cairo, Museum.*

PLATE 72. Quartzite head of a daughter of Akhenaten. Height 8¼ inches; 21 cm.
Cairo, Museum.

PLATE 73. Ruins of the temple of Queen Hatshepsut at Deir el-Bahri.
Eighteenth Dynasty.

PLATE 74. Façade of the rock temple of Ramesses II at Abu Simbel.
Nineteenth Dynasty.

PLATE 75. Protohistoric stone vases from Sakkâra.

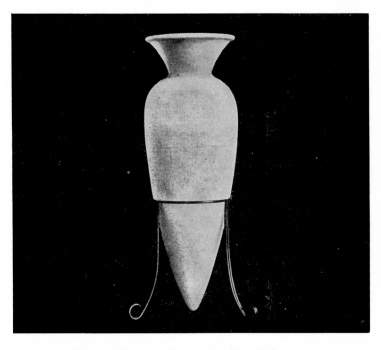

PLATE 76. Large vase in aragonite. First (?) Dynasty.
London, Burlington Fine Arts Club.

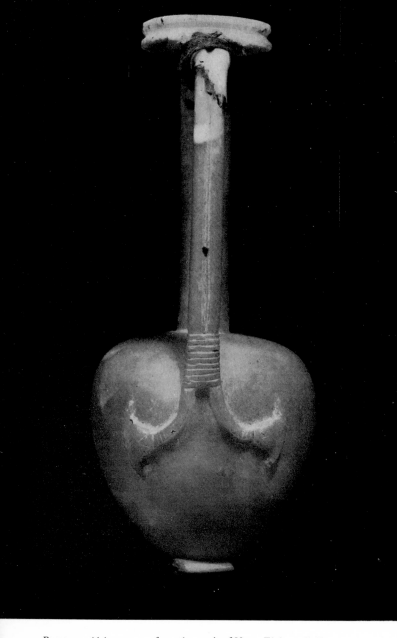

PLATE 77. Alabaster vase from the tomb of Yuya. Eighteenth Dynasty.
Cairo, Museum.

PLATE 78.
Alabaster figurine from
the treasure of Tutankh-
amun. Height about
11¾ inches; 30 cm.
Cairo, Museum.

PLATE 79. Alabaster lamp of the floral type. From the treasure of Tutankhamun. Height 11 inches; 28 cm. *Cairo, Museum*.

PLATE 80. Hippopotamus in faience. New Kingdom. Height 4 inches; 10 cm.
Cairo, Museum.

PLATE 81. Bottles made of polychrome vitreous paste. Eighteenth Dynasty.
Cairo, Museum.

PLATE 82. Yuya's chariot. Length about 110 inches; 280 cm. Eighteenth Dynasty.
Cairo, Museum.

PLATE 83. Funerary mask in stuccoed and painted wood. New Kingdom.
Height of original 9½ inches; 24 cm. *Private Collection.*

PLATE 84. Throne of Tutankhamun. *Cairo, Museum.*

PLATE 85. Model soldiers of Prince Mesehty. Stuccoed and painted wood. From Asyût. Twelfth Dynasty. *Cairo, Museum.*

PLATE 86. Box in the shape of a goose belonging to Princess Sit-Hathor-Merit. From Dahshûr. Twelfth Dynasty. *Cairo, Museum.*

PLATE 87. Cosmetics spoon with floral motive. From Sakkâra.
Eighteenth Dynasty. *Cairo, Museum.*

pounds of bronze in the form of stars and mounds on which the conquering Cross has been placed.

The study of the ritual conceptions connecting obelisks with the custom prevalent among primitive peoples of erecting stones of the menhir and dolmen type, with a substratum of phallic beliefs, lies completely outside the scope of this volume.

To return to the pyramids, the custom of erecting them lasted until after the end of the Old Kingdom. After the dark interlude of the Revolution, under the Eleventh Dynasty, the Middle Kingdom produced the interesting temple of King Montuhotep at Deir el-Bahri, which displays several architectural novelties. In the first place, the 'sacred way' is not covered and is adorned with statues of the king in the shape of Osiris—a clear affirmation of the victory of the god of the poor. The temple as a whole consists of two terraces supported by columns, with a massive stone pyramid rising from the upper terrace.

In certain respects Amenemhet I drew his inspiration from this temple when he built his own. Nevertheless, the layout of the Twelfth Dynasty pyramids differs from those of the Old Kingdom in that it consists of a series of main walls of crude brick with a cruciform ground-plan, intersected by secondary walls, the intervening spaces being filled with fragments of limestone, earth and sand. Sesostris I, Amenemhet II and Sesostris II all built pyramids, and in that of the last-named king was found the only gold *uraeus* from a royal crown that has come down to us. Whereas the first of the above-mentioned pyramids were erected at el-Lisht, which was the royal necropolis at the beginning of the Middle Kingdom, that of Amenemhet II was built at Dahshûr, where Sesostris III and Amenemhet III also erected their pyramids. Sesostris II preferred to erect his at el-Lahûn or 'Illahûn'. Amenemhet III, in addition to the pyramid at Dahshûr, built another one at Hawara.

Little is left of the pyramid of Amenemhet IV at Mazghuna, between Memphis and Fayyûm, the superstructure of which has almost completely disappeared. During the Thirteenth Dynasty Egypt was gradually invaded by the Hyksos 'shepherd kings'. To this period would seem to belong the pyramid recently discovered (in June 1957) at Dahshûr. Inscriptions on the alabaster canopies near the sarcophagus attribute it to a hitherto unknown king, 'Ameni Amu' ('Ameni the Asiatic'). Not far from Sakkâra there are two royal pyramids belonging to the Thirteenth Dynasty. One of these is anonymous and was probably never finished; the other belonged to King Khendjer, who seems to have been the ruler only of the northern portion of the country. It was built of crude bricks, without any casing, and each of its sides is 137 feet long. In all these there is a notable regression compared with the Old Kingdom prototypes; we have, in fact, arrived at the point where the parabola of this architectural form has begun to descend, at all events as regards monumental appearance. It was revived in the private tombs of the New Kingdom, thus perpetuating a tradition going back to the Fifth and Sixth Dynasty necropolises at Abydos, where private individuals erected little pyramids 15 to 20 feet high on parallelepiped bases, inside which the sepulchral chamber was built, the whole being of crude bricks. The type evolved during the New Kingdom was more complicated: the architectural ensemble had many affinities with the houses of the living, but there was also a chapel on which stood a brick pyramid. The last Egyptian king to have a pyramid built for himself, at Abydos, was probably Amosis I.

Under the New Kingdom, temple architecture was substantially modified. The funerary temples were no longer built in the vicinity of the tombs, but their dimensions became considerably larger. Their construction demanded a number of preliminary operations in which the sovereign himself took part. We have already seen how the latter, using a special instrument, played a part in the orientation of the temple; this was followed by the placing of stakes, the purification of the site, the insertion in the foundations of sacred objects in order to keep evil spirits at a distance. All this was regulated by a ceremonial which has been handed down to us on the walls of temples of the Ptolemaic era.

An interesting document, the Papyrus Salt 825 now in the British Museum, gives the rules for the building of the 'House of Life', an important institution of a religious and magical character, in which an appropriate body of priests celebrated special rites and devoted themselves to the compilation of sacred texts. The passage reads as follows: 'As for the "House of Life", it shall be in Abydos. Consisting of four parts, the innermost shall be covered with branches. The "living being" shall be Osiris, while the walls shall be Isis, Nephthys, Horus and Thoth. These are the four sides. Geb [god of the Earth] shall be its floor and Nut [goddess of Heaven] its ceiling. The *being hidden within it* shall be the Great God. The four external bodies shall be of stone, and the floor of sand, while four doors shall open: one to the south, one to the north, one to the west and one to the east. It shall be in a hidden place and spacious. It shall be neither known nor seen, but the sun shall look upon its mysteries. . . .' The papyrus also contains a schematic plan of such a building, the component parts of which were, as we have seen, consecrated to divinities, in particular to those connected with Osiris. An interesting detail is the absence of a ceiling, the place of which was taken by the sky, so that the sun could look upon the 'mysteries' that took place in the building. The temple of Aten at Amarna was also planned to be open to the sun's rays and as a general rule the ancient Egyptians always tried to produce as far as possible the effect of an open sky, even in buildings which had necessarily to be enclosed. The ceiling of the 'sacred way' of Unis at Sakkâra has reproductions of yellow stars on a blue ground, like many chapels of later periods, in which, among other things, the floral columns were designed to heighten the impression of being in the open air. In this conception there is a survival of the innate love for Nature professed by Egyptians from the very beginning of their history.

The most important temple complex dating from the early years of the New Kingdom is certainly that of Queen Hatshepsut at Deir el-Bahri (Plate 73), not far from the temple of Montuhotep which we have already mentioned.

One of the chief merits of the queen's architect, her favourite Senmut, was his artistic exploitation of the natural rocky hemicycle, which in itself is most impressive. The suggestiveness of the bare, perpendicular cliffs is heightened by the phosphorescence of the sun's rays which reflect golden sparks from the rocks and sand. Three terraces one above the other, supported by colonnades, rise gradually to the natural rock wall, while a valley temple, now practically inexistent, was joined to the main temple by a 'sacred way', flanked with sphinxes reproducing the queen's features. The 'sacred way' ended in a lower courtyard, from which a ramp led to the upper courtyard, and in front of this ramp two T-shaped basins were built, in which faïence boomerangs have been found, leading one to suppose that ritual hunts were held in them.

The lower courtyard is surrounded by a limestone perimeter wall and has colonnades on either side of the ramp. Here for the first time we find pillars of a very unusual type: square outside and rounded on the inner side. But here we do not intend to study details, here everything has spatial value, an airiness giving the whole edifice a grandiose aspect. The flat terraces seem to be rising on account of the sloping ramps, while the play of fluted columns breaks the brutality of the surrounding rocks, transforming the temple into a jewel, like a pearl in the rough shell of an oyster.

In the second courtyard, the chapel dedicated to Hathor has the typical columns peculiar to this goddess, whose head, surmounted by a shrine, serves as capital. Lastly, on the upper terrace, whence the eye roves over the Theban countryside intersected by the Nile, stands the actual sanctuary.

Of the scenes adorning the walls of the temple we have already spoken; here we will only mention that they were derived from Old Kingdom models, though this does not in any way reflect on the highly original architectural talent displayed by Senmut.

The evolution of temple architecture during the New Kingdom showed a progressive tendency towards the massive, towards complexes essentially far removed from the grandeur of the pure geometrical forms achieved by the pyramids of the Old Kingdom or from the sober lines of their temples. A typical feature of the new phase in architecture is the construction of great pylons to mark the entrance to the temple, sometimes preceded by an avenue of sphinxes. In front of the pylons stood flagstaffs, an inheritance from the days of the *Iteret* or archaic sanctuary. The colonnades surrounding the courtyards and the hypostyle halls become enormous and more complicated. To the original edifice planned by a Pharaoh his successors added new wings, intersecting each other and superimposed on the earlier buildings. The pillars themselves, enormous, with the figure of the king in the shape of Osiris, accentuate the sense of stability. Little remains of the temple of Tuthmosis III to the north of the Ramesseum, but the pylons and the perimeter wall appear to have been of brick. The last Theban funerary temples of the Eighteenth Dynasty drew their inspiration from the architectonic principles laid down by Senmut at Deir el-Bahri.

A temple complex which, despite the many alterations, presents a uniform aspect, is that of Luxor. Of the original sanctuary, which had probably existed on the same site since the Middle Kingdom, not a trace remains. Obviously all the material that could be utilized was employed by Amenophis III in the construction of the new temple. The layout comprises a first courtyard dating from the days of Ramesses II, who added it to the existing buildings, though it deviates to the east in relationship to the main axis of the temple, since it was necessary to respect the neighbouring shrine of the sacred boats built by Tuthmosis III. To Amenophis III we owe the construction of the actual 'sancta sanctorum', which is preceded by a hypostyle hall and by a large courtyard surrounded by a double row of papyriform columns. This division into three parts is in accordance with religious ideas and implies a selective division of the faithful. The large court was that part of the temple to which all worshippers had access, though they could not go beyond it, since there was a first sanctuary at the extremity of the public portion consisting of five chapels adorned with statues. The intermediate portion of the temple was reserved for the 'middle class', while only priests of high rank could enter the real sanctuary at the far end of the temple, where rites were celebrated before the chief statue of the god. The sobriety of the temple at Luxor, although it shows signs of the increasing heaviness typical of the period in which it was built, gives the architectural ensemble a harmonious and dignified character. In front of the pylon at the entrance Ramesses erected two obelisks of pink granite: one of these, 75 feet high without counting the pedestal, now stands in the Place de la Concorde in Paris; the other, also without counting the pedestal, is 82 feet high.

To Amenophis III, founder of the temple in Luxor, are also due the famous 'colossi of Memnon', which are about 56 feet high and stand on the edge of the cultivated area, giving the landscape a very peculiar aspect. The imagination of the Greeks created an aura of legend round these statues, which made them famous in the eyes of all the travellers of Antiquity. They were then standing at the entrance to a temple dedicated to the same king, later destroyed by an earthquake in the year A.D. 27, as recorded by Strabo.

To have one's own image made in the form of colossal statues, a veritable elephantiasis of stone, denotes a megalomaniac affirmation of the king's individuality at the time when the spiritual background was in decline. By their physical size alone these statues reduced the citizens to subjection to an extent which could no longer be imposed by the respect inherent in the idea of 'sacred' kingship. The theocracy of the Old Kingdom could dispense with colossal statues, and even though funerary architecture evolved those mountains of stone in geometrical form—the pyramids—royal statuary remained aloof, in aristocratic isolation, scorning all compromise with the masses. The rock temple of Abu Simbel, built by Ramesses II, follows in the wake of these colossal statues. Against the levelled wall of rock stand the four figures of the king (Plate 74), 66 feet high, all in the same pose. Ramesses is shown seated on his throne with both arms resting on his thighs, while at his feet, in tiny proportions, are statues of various members of his family. The static effect of these colossi is heightened by the enormous, almost shapeless, pillars represented by the legs, coarsely carved without any trace of muscular plasticity. In the early years of the Middle Kingdom legs of this type had already been made for the statue of Montuhotep, but at that time Egyptian sculpture was emerging from the dark days of the First Intermediate period and the artists had to regain mastery of their tools. Here, on the other hand, we are in a period during which the most delicate Baroque prevailed in every possible form of expression and in which the technique of the chisel delighted in reproducing even the smallest details. The dynamic power of the human figure as found in bas-reliefs and sculptures has ceased to exist in these colossi. The reason for this has already been mentioned: it was the psychological predominance of size by sheer height. And this feeling persists when we enter the hypostyle hall of this temple, in which a row of Osiride pillars more than 30 feet high reproduces the features of the king.

The evolution of 'rock' temples was more successful in Nubia than it was in Egypt. It may be true that rock tombs existed at Gizeh during the Fourth Dynasty and were a characteristic of the Middle Kingdom in Upper Egypt, but the development of rock-temple architecture was almost without significance. Merneptah erected a chapel dedicated to Hathor in the eighteenth *nome* of Upper Egypt, while Hatshepsut and Tuthmosis III built a similar chapel at Beni-Hasan, known as the *speos Artemidos* and important on account of its historical inscriptions. There is also a chapel near Akhmim dedicated by King Ay to the god Min and one at Gebel Silsileh built by Haremhab, these being the last buildings of this type.

But the 'temple city' *par excellence* in Egypt is undoubtedly Karnak, in the neighbourhood of Thebes. Here the sovereigns of the New Kingdom—except during the hiatus of the Akhenaten regime—vied with one another in glorifying Amun, the national divinity, by means of architecture. An inscription tells us of the existence on this site of a temple belonging to the First Intermediate period, while there are various fragments of sacred edifices dating from the Middle Kingdom. The most glorious period for the whole of the area began with Amenophis I, developing further under Tuthmosis I, Hatshepsut and Tuthmosis III, with a profusion of walls and pillars, some of them of the heraldic order, others Osiride, while Hatshepsut's obelisks were also erected. The temple zone was transformed into a veritable mosaic of buildings, grafted one upon the other, and as a result of the continual alterations the ponderous stone architecture became strangely fluid. Amenophis III, Akhenaten's father, made a notable contribution to the development of architecture, followed—after the hiatus caused by the reign of his son—by Sethos I and Ramesses II. The end of the New Kingdom coincided with the beginnings of decadence and Karnak lived on solely on account of its glorious past. Here we cannot pause to make a specific study of this city of temples which forms such an admirable synthesis of the age that produced it. We can, however, quote once again the maxim of King Khety: 'Erect monuments to the gods, so that the name of the builder may live again.' And Karnak is in reality a royal self-glorification, despite the fact that it is dedicated to Amun. The influence of Akhenaten did not make itself felt at Karnak in the form of adoption of stylistic models or ideas from Amarna by his successors, but the surviving remnant of the traditional Pharaonic spirit, still existing in the days of the schismatic king, had been dealt a mortal blow from which it never recovered, and the temple architecture of Sethos I and Ramesses II is a clear proof of this. The columns with their hieroglyphic texts and hollowed-out scenes were rendered heavier by a Baroque trend, and the sober elegance still perceptible in the temple of Amenophis III at Luxor no longer exists.

The reaction of the priests of Amun to the temple of Aten at Amarna was violent. But we possess its exact ground-plan thanks to the reproductions on tombs and above all owing to the tracings left on the site by the old architects, for every component part was marked out on the ground with lines of ink on a foundation of white plaster. Excavations have brought to light these faint outlines, still existing beneath the foundations of the demolished walls.

The Amarna temple differed radically from the classical buildings of the kind that preceded it. It consisted of a rectangle measuring 262 by 84 feet, with the entrance on the west side, perpendicular, as regards its axis, to the royal palace.

It is characterized by the fact that it is almost completely open to the sky, in order to receive the maximum rays of Aten, the 'solar disc', and consists essentially of a series of courts separated by pylons, crammed with offering tables on which the faithful dedicated their gifts to the god. The sanctuary was at the far end of the temple and was flanked by four large statues of Akhenaten, another reminder of the way in which the egocentric iconoclasm of the sovereign, while prohibiting images of other divinities with the exception of the solar disc, found its compensation in the invariable presence of statues of the king himself.

This panorama of temple architecture during the various periods of Egyptian history, though necessarily limited, is based on the considerable number of relics still on the spot, and for this reason it has been given precedence in this chapter. The relics of civil and military architecture are far less numerous. Military architecture has no artistic importance: as in the case of most old civilizations, it was limited to purely functional defensive walls and bastions. We will confine ourselves to mentioning the fortresses of Ikkur, Kuban and Aniba, formerly attributed to the Old Kingdom, but later to the Eleventh and Twelfth Dynasties, with their double belts of brick walls. The fort at Khor, on the other hand, has triple walls, showing that they were constructed in successive stages. Noteworthy by reason of their size are the forts at Matuka and Semneh el-Gharb, where the perimeter walls are broken by protruding bastions giving complete control of the surrounding zone. But, as we have already said, these buildings, though interesting from the technical and historical standpoint, are outside the range of the present volume. The only civil dwelling-house of Old Kingdom times was discovered by Lauer in Zoser's perimeter wall and dates from the Third Dynasty: built of crude bricks, all that remains of it is the very simple ground-plan. Another testimony to the activities of artists at this time is provided by an *ostrakon* in the museum at Cairo, with co-ordinates expressed in cubits, palms and digits, referring to the diagram of a vault very similar to that of a Third Dynasty building near the ruins of which the *ostrakon* itself was found. The little terracotta models known as 'houses of the spirit' are found in large numbers in the superstructures of tombs dating from the Sixth to the Twelfth Dynasty. They reproduce with gradual improvements the dwelling-houses of the living and show a real evolution in the art of building.

Consisting sometimes of two stories with rooms opening out of a vestibule and often adorned with columns, these facsimiles of homes were later embellished with little models of domestic furniture. The tomb of Meketrē', of the Eleventh Dynasty, has a remarkable variety of such models executed in wood, to which we shall return when we deal with the 'Minor Arts'. The houses of the upper classes were distinguished by a perimeter wall enclosing a garden, embellished with plants and a pool. The village of Kahun, excavated by Petrie and dating from the Middle Kingdom, had upper-class houses with a complicated ground-plan. They stood at the eastern end of the village, separated by a brick wall from the west side, which contained the more modest dwellings. Ricke has made a detailed study of the structure of various dwellings and it is interesting to examine the ground-plan of one of the largest. The entrance was guarded by a doorkeeper, who had his own lodge on one side of it. Two antechambers, their ceilings borne by columns, preceded the courtyard and were connected with each other by a long gallery. From the second antechamber access was gained to the court, adorned with a portico with nine columns, and from this presumably started the staircase leading up to the terrace, while two doors led respectively to the women's quarters (harem) and the room of the master. The latter was in its turn preceded by a square vestibule, the ceiling of which was borne by four columns, flanked by a little hall with two columns and the bedroom, of which the alcove has been preserved. Other rooms followed from south to west as far as the bathroom. The harem consisted of a square hall with twelve columns, probably an open court with colonnades on all four sides, with a cistern in the middle. The other rooms of this part of the house ran from north to south and included rooms for the servants, while the kitchens and annexes were on the south-east side. The house consisted of seventy rooms and covered an area measuring 196 by 148 feet. The walls were whitewashed and covered with paintings, but unfortunately no scene worth mentioning has survived.

Under the New Kingdom, the dwelling-houses became larger and were provided with 'comforts', since this was a period of luxury in which the holding of frequent receptions made it necessary that they should be completely furnished. The houses of Tell el-Amarna, the city built by Akhenaten, generally had a square ground-plan, with imposing entrances and ceilings supported by a central column, or, more rarely, two. The internal rooms varied according to the owner's standing, but were generally characterized by the sharp distinction drawn between reception-rooms and the more intimate living-rooms, a feature still noticeable in the private houses of the East. Under the New Kingdom special attention was paid to the gardens; flowers were usually offered to the guests by a maid during receptions.

The working-class homes, known to us from Tell el-Amarna and Deir el-Medîneh, were naturally much simpler, but invariably decent. A reception-room led into the parlour, from which access was gained to the bedroom and kitchen. Many houses had granaries, circular at Amarna and rectangular at Deir el-Medîneh; such granaries are also to be found in the annexes of upper-class dwellings. From the study of what has come down to us concerning Egyptian towns we can affirm that the ancient inhabitants of the Nile Valley, despite the changes inevitable in the course of three thousand years, created a domestic architecture which was rational but at the same time in good taste, achieving a compromise between simplicity and refinement.

CHAPTER NINE

The minor arts

U NDER the generic term of 'minor arts' we have grouped together the crafts and industrial activities of the ancient Egyptians. In the preceding pages we have considered certain aspects of the 'major arts'— architecture, sculpture, painting—forms of expression which were influenced, if not actually conditioned, by religious conceptions and the finalism of the Netherworld.

The field we are about to examine freed itself from such limitations. The creative artistic spirit of the ancient Egyptians was, in fact, more freely expressed in craftsmanship than elsewhere. In studying its products we are struck, not so much by the technical skill, as by the aesthetical factor, sometimes exquisite and harmonious in its forms, so that the object becomes more and more an expression of a people or of a given time, and achieves the immanence of beauty.

This leads us to an axiomatic preliminary consideration: even in the production of common articles for everyday use, quite apart from their functionality, the craftsmen of the Pharaonic civilization strove to express the maximum of aesthetic achievement. Craftsman and customer were bound together by the link of good taste, so that supply and demand, by stimulating each other reciprocally, prevented any decadence of 'style' and determined, as a result of emulation, the creation of new forms of artistic expression by the craftsmen.

POTTERY

This is one of the oldest industrial activities, as is proved by the finds in pre-dynastic cemeteries, where clay vases, plain or painted, have been discovered in large quantities. In those early days pottery was considered a 'luxury' and was therefore sparingly used. With the advent of the Thinite era its use became general, and pottery therefore lost its original rarity value. The raw material was more or less light-coloured Nile clay and the shape was obtained with the aid of the classical wheel, known as *nehep*, which was rotated by the left hand while the right modelled the surfaces of the vase. The god Chnum, patron of the potters, is sometimes represented with a ram's head while performing this function, since he was one of the divinities who 'modelled' the human race, using clay as his raw material. The god Ptah was also believed to be a patron of this art, as well as of sculpture. A text from Edfu describes him as 'the sculptor of sculptors, the potter of potters'.

In Middle Kingdom tombs we often find scenes illustrating the various phases of the craft: we see the potters preparing the raw material by treading it with their feet, in order to expel the moisture present in the clay and at the same time obtain a homogeneous paste; others are seen working at the wheel, giving the clay different shapes in accordance with the requirements and tastes of their customers. Others again are seen placing the already modelled articles on top of a rather high kiln, the fuel used consisting of wood. It is interesting to note that a kiln of this type was called a *ta*, a term having the same phonetic value as the word for 'earth', with which it was evidently connected in men's minds.

During the archaic period pottery was fired only to a limited extent and the same may be said of the red colouring obtained by using haematite. Nevertheless, it was at this time that the more or less classical forms were established, although later periods, in particular the New Kingdom, also contributed their characteristic imprint, since they were periods of luxury and refinement.

The generic term for 'vase' in Egyptian is *henu*, but there are many variants according to the purposes for which the articles were intended. For example, *mer* means a jar used for carrying milk, while *remnet*, *niu* and *djadjau* denote jars for medicines. The last of these terms was also used to denote a censer or a pot containing honey, or as a unit of capacity. On the other hand, the large vases so often found in the mural paintings in tombs were called *sunu*. They were intended to contain both liquids such as wine and beer, and dry articles, and the reddish terracotta ground is often adorned with floral motives or bunches of grapes, and even horses. Examples of this type are reproduced in the tomb of Userhat, who lived in the reign of Amenophis II, and in Berlin there is one 17 inches high with an interesting representation of a horse. All these large vases, the bottoms of which were either curved or pointed, could be carried with the aid of special supports consisting of wooden poles.

A classification according to types, based on the study made by Reisner and on the finds at Naga ed-Deir and Tura, groups the various categories of the oldest vases into seven main classes, with an additional class for special cases. Obviously, the types included in these classes may differ widely among each other as regards size, and also, to a slight extent, in shape. Petrie's classification is far more complex, since he also considers as classes the sub-categories of each specific type. We think it will help the reader if we give below a summary of the principal categories.

First group. This is characterized by the elongated form, wider at the top, sometimes decorated with a border in relief, and shaped at the bottom like a truncated cone. To this class belong, in particular, the jars used for holding grain and beer.

Second group. Here the sides are invariably curved and the bottom flat, pointed or round. Though the shape is somewhat elongated, the vases of this group lack the buoyant thrust of the first.

Third group. This group comprises vases distinguished by a tendency to become almost swollen at the top, while the bottom is either round or flat, never pointed.

Fourth group. The sides of the vases are more or less convex. The bottom, invariably flat, always has the same breadth as the rim, while the shape of the body varies between the cylindrical and the ovoid.

Fifth group. Characterized by the cylindrical shape, particularly frequent at Tura; sides generally straight, but sometimes concave or even convex. To this group also belong the vases known as 'Libyan', with slightly rounded bottoms.

Sixth group. Globular and spherical vases, somewhat rare. More frequent at Tura than at Naga ed-Deir.

Seventh group. With flat bottoms and convex, or occasionally rectilinear, sides and semi-spherical bodies. Some specimens have a spout for pouring out liquids. The lowest types look like cups.

Eighth group. Comprises special cases which cannot be assigned to any of the above groups. A comparison of the types studied by Junker and Reisner reveals that there are more typological variants at Tura. For example, vases with spouts, ovoid vases, conical vases, etc.

In addition to the vases made of clay, during the prehistoric period—somewhere around Petrie's 'sequence date 64'—stone vases came into general use. Far more complicated as regards technique, the fashioning of hard stone required different equipment and truly admirable patience. The raw materials used varied greatly: alabaster, slate, basalt, limestone, diorite, porphyry, syenite and rock-crystal (Plates 75, 76). When discussing stone statuary, we mentioned the technique and instruments used in making such works. In the specific case of the stone-vase maker's art, after choosing his block and squaring it roughly, the craftsman proceeded to hollow it out with the aid of a special gimlet. That this craft is one of the oldest practised by man is proved by the fact that the gimlet used for such work later became the ideographic sign for 'art' in general.

The finishing, which was done with emery, often achieved an unrivalled degree of perfection, and the craftsmen contrived to make the sides of the vases so thin that they almost resembled transparent foil.

For stone vases there exists a typological classification into five main groups, instead of eight as in the case of clay vases.

First group. Includes vases made for the most part of alabaster and limestone. The shape is cylindrical with rectilinear sides, either concave or convex, sometimes narrowing towards the top. Some items bear an ornamental motive imitating a rope or sinuous line. Rare, on the other hand, is the presence of little 'ears' at the sides, like tiny handles.

Second group. Includes various types: spherical, pear-shaped and barrel-shaped. The last-named has convex walls sometimes narrowing at the base. All the vases of this category have rims, and in the case of the semi-spherical containers they sometimes possess the characteristic of being composed of two sections, fitted together horizontally, after being hollowed out separately.

Third group. Characterized by slender, but not cylindrical, shapes, with double-curved sides and the rudiments of a neck.

Fourth group. This is the category of bowls and similar vessels, with usually convex sides and flat bottoms. Only in exceptional cases are the sides concave. It should be noted that some bowls have such low sides that they are almost plates.

Fifth group. This corresponds to the eighth group of clay vases and includes the special cases. To this category belong the pieces found by Junker at Tura and others coming from the excavations at Helwan, noteworthy examples being an alabaster goblet and a perfume-vase of the type often depicted in the hands of a maidservant at receptions. In the tomb of the vizier Hemaka at Sakkâra a number of stands were found for keeping round- or pointed-bottomed vases upright.

Among the raw materials used for making vases during the various periods, alabaster long maintained a privileged place, since it was generally used for luxury articles and was admirably suited for decoration (Plate 77). Goblets, lamps and precious caskets bear witness to the skill achieved by craftsmen in handling this material, and some beautiful items were found in the tomb of Tutankhamun (Plates 78, 79). This monarch's canopic vases (for holding entrails) were made of alabaster and his effigy is admirably reproduced on their lids. Here the art of the potter was combined with that of the sculptor and with the production of luxurious *bibelots*, but it must be remembered that the workshops were run on collective lines and each man's special job was clearly defined. The craftsman who made the 'body' of the canopic vase, for example, was not necessarily the same man who made the anthropo- or zoo-cephalic lids. This also applies to all similar cases and for that matter we have already seen how several artists worked together on a single statue or on a boat, a definite task being assigned to each of them.

A typical 'funerary' vase was produced by making copies in painted clay of originals executed in precious materials. Here the same rule of magic applied, which put the reproduction on the same plane as the original object. Thus in the Fifth Dynasty pyramid of King Neferirkarē' a gilded wooden vase inlaid with vitreous pastes reproduces a magnificent specimen of goldsmith's work, while in the tomb of Yuya and Tuyu, Akhenaten's grandparents, a series of painted earthenware vases consists of imitations of alabaster and other precious stones. From the first dynasties onwards we find vessels made of hard stone used exclusively for funerary purposes. In fact, while the external aspect coincided with that of similar articles intended for the living, the interior reveals only a trace of hollowing out, and what remains is in reality a solid and heavy block. The vases imitating Cretan ceramics now in the museum at Liverpool date from the Middle Kingdom.

Alabaster asserted itself in vases destined for use during funeral rites, among them being those containing the seven 'sacred' oils. Theriomorphic vases, i.e. those in the shapes of animals, are found during all periods. A curious example, now in the Metropolitan Museum at New York and dating from the Sixth Dynasty, shows a female monkey with her baby clinging to her. Other pieces reproduce geese, these being among the most important funerary offerings.

Many paintings, especially those of the New Kingdom, show vases being carried as tributes or being offered to the gods, but generally such pieces were executed in precious metals and thus belong to the art of the goldsmith rather than to that of the stone-vase maker. In pre-dynastic times vases appear with traces of glazing, e.g. clay vases, portions of which are covered with a bluish-green vitreous glaze. In more remote times this glaze seems to have been limited to small ornamental objects such as the beads intended for use in trinkets. In the First Dynasty tomb of King Udimu, Petrie found fragments of vases, as well as others in a better state of preservation, covered with a blue glaze. Fragments dating from the reign of Semerkhet reveal a shade tending towards violet. The study of this new material leads us directly to that of its origin and production.

FAÏENCE

This technical term is derived from the name of the Italian city of Faenza, where, from 1480 on, a type of porcelain was produced with a glaze of a uniform brilliant blue, similar in tone to that of the objects found in Pharaonic tombs.

The corresponding Egyptian term used from the days of the Old Kingdom was *thehenet*, which also denotes coloured vitreous paste. Its hieroglyph consists of a pendant of beads, and in fact these beads are the oldest evidence of its use.

Newberry connects the word *thehenet* with *Thehenu*,

which denoted the north-western zone of the Delta, where it was presumably first used and became known. This is supported by the fact that the alkalis forming part of this substance came for the most part from the Wadi Natrûn, situated in that area.

The discovery of this compound was probably quite accidental; the quartzose sand melted by the bivouac fires in the presence of some cuprous mineral produced a glittering mass with beautiful coloured iridescences. Pieces subjected to analysis reveal a compact mass consisting of powdered grains of quartz, and it is almost certain that the pulverization was obtained by artificial means. The adhesive 'medium' was the *natron* or carbonate of soda found in the Wadi Natrûn. Lucas, to whom we owe the chief studies in this field, obtained a compound very similar to old faïence by melting, at a fairly high temperature, powdered quartz mixed with 10 per cent of *natron*. The starting-point, both for faïence and for vitreous pastes, is therefore the same: the melting down of siliceous sand with a mineral colouring agent. This probably explains why the same term is used to denote both products.

The colouring materials responsible for the superficial 'vitrification' were minerals such as copper, cobalt, manganese and ferrous alloys. The usual colour produced by these was blue in all its chromatic variations down to green: tones corresponding to turquoise, beryl and feldspar green. The choice of colour can hardly have been due to chance or faulty workmanship, since examples of other colours have been preserved. It was probably based on some magical notion which attributed thaumaturgical effects to particular shades.

And in fact nearly all amulets representing divinities or sacred animals were made of greenish-blue faïence, which in New Kingdom times was also used for one of the types of *ushabti*, or funerary figurines of servants. Of the same material were the ritual boomerangs used in ceremonies in the temple pools, such as those found in the temple of Queen Hatshepsut at Deir el-Bahri. The blue glaze has a lighter tone during the Eleventh and Twelfth Dynasties, and deepens in intensity after the Second Theban Epoch (Eighteenth Dynasty), until it reaches the magnificent blue shade known as 'Deir el-Bahri' from the place where most of the examples were found. This tone is obtained by using colours based on copper and cobalt, while the inscriptions and decorative motives were executed with derivatives of manganese.

The famous 'blue rooms' of the Third Dynasty tomb of King Zoser at Sakkâra have on their walls hundreds of blue faïence tiles representing wattle work. Little models of lotus-bud and papyriform columns, replicas of funerary offerings—especially fruit and vegetables—abound during the Middle and New Kingdom periods. During the Middle Kingdom somewhat caricaturish renderings of hippopotami are often found, the aquatic plants among which these animals live being painted on their bodies—the *Nymphaea lotus*, the *Nymphaea caerulea* and the *Potamogeton lucens*—sometimes with little birds perched on their stems. This is an interesting case of 'projection' on to an animal's body of elements forming part of its habitat. The hippopotamus is, in fact, depicted crossing a pond, surrounded by plants through which he makes his way. Since he did not know how to represent such a scene in any other way, the Egyptian artist had recourse to the ingenious expedient of painting it *sic et simpliciter* on the animal's body (Plate 80).

In the same way as the boomerangs other weapons were reproduced in faïence, for example the Twelfth Dynasty club found at el-Lisht.

Faïence was also very suitable for the making of funerary jewels. Tubular elements of this material were used to make the collars known as *uesekh*, or 'broad', which were hung round the necks of mummies, and also for the funerary rings and figures of genii placed among the wrappings. At a later period the mummy, swathed in linen wrappings, was covered with a 'network' consisting of tubular elements in blue faïence. All these articles were made in terracotta moulds into which the still incandescent mass was poured, the finishing touches being then made as required. Thousands of these moulds have come down to us, and it has even been possible to identify certain 'pieces' with the moulds in which they were cast.

During the New Kingdom era blue faïence was used to make very elegant goblets reproducing the form of the lotus, and for bowls which the imagination of the artists provided with beautiful decorations, the patterns used being geometrico-floral, zoological or erotico-bucolic. The last-named were the most frequent and often reproduced a naked girl playing a lute or steering a fragile boat through a papyrus-thicket. The sense of humour which, as we have already seen, was prominently displayed in the *ostraka* from Deir el-Medîneh, is found again in the decorations adorning these bowls. By a reversal of the normal situation, a monkey is depicted compelling his master to dance.

Some examples of this category reveal highly original ideas, e.g. the 'Massimo Campigli' heads on the bowl now in the museum at Turin (Plate I).

In all these compositions the dominant element is a feeling for measure and elegance, geometry being exploited by the artist in order to achieve the maximum aesthetic effect.

Very beautiful scarabs were also made of faïence, but owing to the fragility of this material it was generally replaced by steatite or some other more robust material when it was a question of making seals.

Although, as we have said, faïence was normally used in blue shades, specimens in other colours also exist, e.g. the beautiful perfume phial in the form of an amphora now in the Metropolitan Museum, with its white ground and blue floral ornaments, and the polychrome decorative plaques depicting prisoners from the palace of Ramesses III at Medinet Habu, now in the museum at Cairo.

At a later period the same material was used for imitations of silver vases and bean-shaped flasks, known as 'New Year flasks' owing to the formula inscribed upon them asking the gods to 'open a new year' for the owner. They have necks shaped like a lotus-bud capital, flanked by two monkeys, and all of them date from the Saite period. In the museum at

Berlin there is a flask of this kind which still has its original casing of plaited fibre.

The ancient Egyptians never succeeded in producing real 'porcelain', and their nearest approach to it, faïence, notwithstanding its popularity, never had the same importance for them that porcelain had for the Chinese.

Nevertheless, faïence was one of the most characteristic products of ancient Egypt, and thanks to the Phoenicians it soon became known throughout the Mediterranean basin.

VITREOUS PASTES

We have already said that faïence and vitreous pastes may have had the same origin; in the case of the former, however, 'vitrification' is limited to the surface, whereas in vitreous pastes the whole mass is vitrified.

The colouring is always due to the use of mineral substances and tends as far as possible to imitate the semi-precious stones such as lapis lazuli, and in this respect these pastes belong to the goldsmith's workshop.

Although vitreous fragments exist which have been attributed to the Old and Middle Kingdom periods there is no evidence of any production on a large scale before the Eighteenth Dynasty. The first factory or 'glassworks' of which the ruins have been identified by archaeological research goes back to the reign of Amenophis III in Thebes, but numerous items from earlier periods reveal an already refined technique and an 'industrial' character. The various stages in the development of the art of glass-making can be defined as follows:

Prehistoric. Vitreous elements in ornaments, of small size and often mistaken for faïence.

Early Historic. First Dynasty. Semi-opaque blue vitreous pastes used as inlays in wooden objects found at Abydos and now at the Ashmolean Museum, Oxford. In the tomb of a queen, the wife of King Djer, turquoise-coloured vitreous plaques were found.

Middle Kingdom. Twelfth Dynasty. Vitreous mosaic found by De Morgan at Dahshûr among the jewellery of the princesses of the household of Amenemhet II. This is a polychrome piece of circular shape with a white calf depicted in the centre, the whole being mounted in gold. To the same dynasty can be attributed another mosaic, now in the British Museum, showing the *cartouche* of Amenemhet in white on a black ground.

New Kingdom. The use of vitreous pastes becomes general, especially for goblets, vases, bottles, and decorations for ornamental elements of all kinds. From this period date the little Pharaonic heads made of vitreous paste, among which should be noted those in the Louvre depicting one of the daughters of Akhenaten and a Pharaoh of the late Eighteenth Dynasty. In the latter case the face and wig are in different shades. Another noteworthy item is the blue goblet of Tuthmosis III, now at Munich, with a

dark blue and yellow motive of surrounding lines and
the name of the sovereign inscribed in blue. Other
items of the same type bear the names of Amenophis
II, Amenophis III and Akhenaten. In the schismatic
king's city of Tell el-Amarna four 'glassworks' have
been found, which worked very efficiently during the
comparatively brief existence of the city. The forms,
too, reveal a search for original motives, for example
the fish-shaped polychrome vase found at Amarna.
Other vases draw their inspiration from little palm-
leaf columns or are embellished with elegant handles
and feet adorned with multi-coloured incrustations.
In general, the vases follow alabaster models decorated with sinuous or 'wavy' lines, or with discs and
other geometrical motives, all of them polychrome
(Plate 81).

The process of manufacture was far from simple
and, as happens in the large modern glassworks, e.g.
at Murano, a highly specialized category of workmen
arose who were capable of distinguishing 'by eye' the
degree of heat necessary for the various stages of the
work.

A wrong interpretation of certain Old Kingdom
scenes, showing craftsmen blowing into long reeds
ending in a mass resting on a fire, led many scholars to
affirm that even in those remote days the Egyptians
produced glass articles by blowing. A closer study,
however, has shown that these are metal-workers and
that the technique of glass-blowing was not practised
until the Graeco-Roman period.

Thebes was the capital of the New Kingdom and

the most skilful artisans accordingly flocked to the city. But the production of glass as a raw material would not seem to have been a prerogative of Upper Egypt. According to Newberry it was imported in the form of bars from factories in the Delta. Once they arrived at their destination, these bars were broken up and melted down in special crucibles. When the paste became fluid and viscous it was removed by means of metal pincers and rotated until it assumed the form of tubes of varying diameter or even the form of wire. A mould of sandy clay was then prepared, traversed by a little metal bar which the craftsman held in his hand. Round this mould were wrapped the hot strips of glass, sometimes of various colours, though normally the use of a monochrome foundation was preferred, to which layers of coloured glass were then applied. This mass was then returned to the furnace until the various strips became cohesive, after which the ornamental motives were added; then the vase was once again placed in the furnace, supported by metal pincers, the function of which was to keep the various parts in place. At this point skilful finishing touches impressed the undulating or zigzag motives on the surface, and the vase was then taken out of the furnace for the last time. The last phase consisted of finishing off with emery to remove minor imperfections, and Howard Carter has pointed out that we can often see how the air-bubbles on the vases have been neatly cut away. The insides of the vases generally have rather rough surfaces, this being due to the presence of sand in the mass of clay forming the nucleus. This, as soon as the glass had cooled, was

PLATE 88. Cosmetics spoon. New Kingdom. *Cairo, Museum.*

PLATE 89. Cosmetics spoon. New Kingdom. *Cairo, Museum.*

PLATE 90. Cosmetics spoon. New Kingdom. *Cairo, Museum.*

PLATE 91. Statuette with vase for ointment. Eighteenth Dynasty.
Cairo, Museum.

PLATE 92. Handle of a cosmetics spoon (without basin). New Kingdom.
Cairo, Museum.

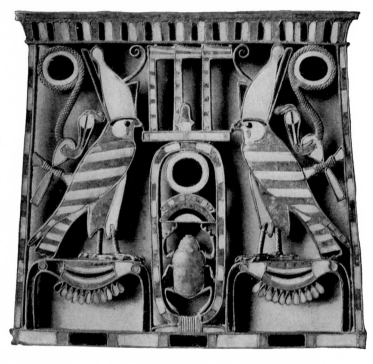

PLATE 93. Pectoral of Sesostris II, in gold and coloured stones.
Height about 2 inches; 5 cm. *Cairo, Museum.*

PLATE 94. Bronze mirror with "Hathorian" handle of ebony, gold and coloured stones, belonging to Princess Sit-Hathor-Yunut, daughter of Sesostris I. From el-Lahûn. *Cairo, Museum.*

PLATE 95. Ceremonial axe of King Amosis I, in gold, ebony and "electrum".
Seventeenth Dynasty. *Cairo, Museum.*

PLATE 96. Ceremonial fan of King Tutankhamun. Chased gold. *Cairo, Museum.*

PLATE 97. Bronze head of a cat. Low Era. Height 3 inches; 7.5 cm.
Private collection.

PLATE 98. Fish of the oxyrhyncus family, in bronze with silver eyes and surmounted by the solar disc between horns. Low Era. Length 4¾ inches; 12 cm.
Private collection.

PLATE 99. Ibis in bronze, with eyes of lapis lazuli. On wooden base. New Kingdom. Length of base 6¼ inches; 16 cm. *Private collection.*

PLATE 100. Statuette of an ichneumon. Low Era. Total length 6 inches; 15 cm. *Private collection.*

PLATE 101. Situla in fused bronze with scenes in relief. Late period. Height 8¾ inches; 22 cm. *Turin, Museum.*

PLATE 102. Situla in thin plate. Height 14½ inches; 36.5 cm.
Eighteenth Dynasty. *Turin, Museum.*

removed with the aid of the metal bar. The foot of the vase, also moulded by heat, was added while the mass was still soft. On the whole the instruments required for this process were very primitive, but they were supplemented by the great skill of the individual craftsmen. At a later period, when Egypt declined and Alexandria began to flourish, the glorious cycle of the art of glass-making returned to its place of origin: the Delta, or *thehenu*. Hadrian and Strabo mention the pre-eminence of Alexandria in this field in their writings.

WOOD-CARVING

The scarcity of wood in Egypt had as a consequence that it was carefully handled when used as a raw material and that the articles produced were reserved for the upper classes. The lower classes, of course, had their wooden furniture, but this was of inferior quality and coarse execution without any of those refinements of inlay which are characteristic of real furniture-making. The oldest royal tombs of the early historical period provide evidence of the use of sumptuous furnishings, though very little has survived. The articles of furniture had carved wooden or ivory feet in imitation of animals' paws, and according to Petrie this usage goes back to 'sequence date 66', denoting the date of a Negadah tomb in which a bed with bull's feet was found. After this period the technique of the inlaying of the various wooden component parts improved and nails were replaced by wooden pins. The 'frame' of the bed was of plaited vegetable fibre, and it should be noted that at Tarkhan during the early historical period people preferred to be buried lying on their beds, rather than in a sarcophagus,

Under the Old Kingdom the art of furniture-making had already achieved artistic maturity: items from the Fourth Dynasty tomb of the mother of King Cheops, among them a litter, are real works of art. Goldsmiths and wood-carvers collaborated, and inlay-work, the use of gems and chasing were adapted to wooden furniture. The hieroglyphs in gold on a black ground which adorn the above-mentioned litter are in reality little jewels, but of greater interest for the purposes of our study is the perfect harmony of the forms. It was natural that in wood-carving, too, various forms of specialization should soon arise: the furniture-maker had in his workshop craftsmen who devoted themselves exclusively to the fashioning of the feet, and others who specialized in inlay-work or in the application of stucco and gilding. Lastly, after the introduction of horses into Egypt, there were crafts-men specialized in the production of wagons, chariots, etc. (Plate 82). Another branch was essentially funerary in character and produced the anthropomorphic sarcophagi so frequently used, especially during the New Kingdom era. In such cases a real sculptor was employed, who gave the funerary mask features closely resembling those of the deceased. Masks of this kind were made either of wood or of *papier mâché*. In the former cases the wood was coated with argillaceous plaster, covered by a layer of chalk which was then painted (Plate 83). The *papier mâché*, on the other hand, consisted of various strata of vegetable fibres glued together and pressed. The work of the painter-decorator was the last creative phase. As in the case of wooden statues, artificial eyes in copper or bronze settings were also used for anthropomorphic sarcophagi. Another sideline in the workshop of the specialist in funerary articles was the production of the ceremonial beds on which the mummy was exhibited to relatives and friends. The sides of these were decorated with mythical figures or images of the gods; interesting specimens of them were found in the tomb of Tutankhamun, the only tomb to yield articles of furniture in large quantities. One of these 'beds' shows the goddess Nut in twofold aspect as the celestial cow, and the craftsman who made it achieved a perfect equilibrium between the parts: the tails balance the horns on the foreheads, while the elongated body gives lightness to the static pose of the animal.

Universally known is the 'throne' of Tutankhamun, made of wood, gold leaf and vitreous pastes (Plate 84). Though with its decorativeness it is almost Baroque, it is nevertheless a stupendous product of that period during which craftsmen were affected by the prevalent craze for gold. Replicas of pieces of furniture of this type have proved that they were reasonably comfortable and that the decorations never detracted from this comfort. This was, in fact, one of the chief characteristics of the art of furniture-making in ancient Egypt. When subjected to a technical analysis, the various items of furniture prove that the requirements of hygiene and comfort came first and that the application of ornamental motives and decorations was subordinated to these. The inlay-work and miniature-painting, found in such abundance under the New Kingdom, reveal an atavistic technique which could only have been acquired after many generations of craftsmen had specialized in one field. One of Tutankhamun's caskets consists of over twenty thousand tiny inlaid pieces of ebony and ivory! Sometimes these elements were imitated by painters, though only as surrounds for painted scenes in which they could display the best of their talents. Generally these were scenes of hunting or war, if the work was destined for a sovereign, but private individuals usually preferred scenes of country life with little girls playing musical instruments and dancing.

The Middle Kingdom witnessed a development in the making of little funerary models in wood. These were statuettes of the 'servants of the deceased' bringing funerary offerings, or troops of soldiers whose duty it was to defend their master in the world to come (Plate 85). Or else they were clever reproductions of scenes such as the inspection of cattle, in which the deceased himself took part, surrounded by his scribes with their account-books. The lifelikeness of these scenes is due to the care with which each single action is reproduced: the gestures of the herdsmen raising their sticks to urge on their animals, the different attitudes of the various personages and the amusing little scene in which a 'culprit' is brought before his master to receive the punishment he deserves. Or again, in the same category, the little models of granaries with people working in them, or of craftsmen's workshops—all of them valuable evidence of actual life at that time. Wood was admirably suited for this kind of art, which reproduces indiscriminately men and animals, dwelling-houses and boats.

This art of modelling, though it reached full development during the Middle Kingdom, had already existed during the Old, but in those days the material used was generally terracotta or limestone. In the corridor of the chapel of Hesirēᶜ there is a graphical rendering of many pieces of furniture and other works by Third Dynasty craftsmen, all conceived in the same spirit as the 'models' we have just discussed.

But where the art of the wood-carver achieved heights of refinement and good taste, such as had never been attained before, was in the creation of articles for the toilet-tables of women, in particular the so-called 'cosmetic spoons'.

The first slate 'palettes' for grinding and mixing rouge made their appearance in pre-dynastic times. Their shapes were very varied: either they took the form of shields with the heads of human beings or animals as ornaments, or they were theriomorphic and reproduced the fauna of the period—elephants, tortoises, birds and fish. This latter type survived into the historical period and generally reproduced, either in stone or in wood, the fish known as the *tilapia nilotica*. These primitive types were used as aids to female beauty, but in historical times their function was taken over by wooden spoons. The spoons of the oldest period, found at Negadah, reveal a constant search for new decorative motives, but they would seem to have been used exclusively as tableware. Only in the days of the New Kingdom did they come into general use as toilet articles for the ladies of the period. According to Capart, the animals reproduced on the oldest examples—geese, antelopes or oxen—were symbolical sacrificial animals, the reproductions being substituted for the animals themselves in accordance with the magical praxis we have already mentioned, these theriomorphic containers being filled with the fat of the animal represented, which was then offered as a sacrifice on the altar.

For us the most interesting are the wooden 'pieces', some of which are real masterpieces of gracefulness. Geese are often represented, as well as certain floral motives in which the calyx and bud form the cavity for the rouge (Plates 86, 87). The stems, on the other hand, are harmonized to form a geometrical pattern, which at the same time serves as a handle. Bucolic scenes were, however, generally preferred by the artist: the 'spoon' has an elongated shape and the portion forming the handle is decorated with little figures of human beings and animals surrounded by aquatic plants (Plates 88, 89). The blue lotus often appears, and sometimes the fruits of the mandrake, papyrus and poppy.

Running water is represented by zigzag lines, as in the example in the museum at Cairo, in which two rowers are conveying a calf in their boat among the high stems of the plants (Plate 90). In this case the handle and the cavity form one compact block, but in most examples the handle is perforated and the human figure stands out much more clearly.

Another theme used on these spoons is that of a manservant or maid bending beneath the weight of a large vessel (Plate 91). Examples of this type can be seen in the museums at Leyden and Cairo and in the Louvre, while the same motive provided inspiration for statuettes, in which the naturalistic attitude and the distortion of the bust are noteworthy.

The figure of the god Bes often appears—a grotesque divinity who was the patron of sleep and was also associated in some way with Hathor, the Goddess of Love. Most of these 'spoons' are made of wood, but there are also examples in ivory and stone. Sometimes the concave part of the spoon is closed by a hinged lid.

Connected with the fundamental bucolico-erotic motive are various notions, one of the most graceful of which is that of the 'swimming girl', whom we have already seen represented on the *ostrakon* preserved in Turin. In ancient Egypt girls often plunged naked into pools or backwaters of the river, to cool themselves or to fish, pushing in front of them a little basin or a duck, which, when the motive was applied to spoons, became the cavity. In Cairo there are several such spoons, among them one, without the basin, in which the girl's body is exquisitely modelled, while the little head, adorned with an elaborate coiffure, emerges, theoretically, above the level of the water (Plate 92). The gathering of plants and flowers, or girls making music, were also favourite themes, but always gracefully rendered. They illustrate passages from the 'love lyrics' which were in vogue at that time:

> My god, my beloved,
> it is sweet to dive
> and swim before thee.
> Thus I show thee my beauty
> in the tunic of finest linen,
> when it is wet.
> I enter the water with thee
> and to thee I return . . .
> A beautiful red fish
> darts between my fingers.
> Oh, come and behold me.

GOLDSMITH'S WORK

The desire for ornaments is a human tendency dating from the remotest prehistoric times. Shells of molluscs, bones, coloured pebbles, were the materials out of which primitive trinkets were fashioned. In Egypt we have evidence of the existence of a primitive manufacture of jewellery during the pre-dynastic era; necklaces and bracelets show that various stones were used: agate, quartz, turquoise, serpentine, lapis lazuli, haematite, carnelian, chalcedony. At the time of the First Dynasty jewels become numerous and of varied forms. Petrie found four bracelets on a mummified arm in the 'cenotaph' of King Djer at Abydos. One of these consisted of alternate gold and turquoise plaques representing the façade of the royal palace, surmounted by the falcon. Isolated pieces in ivory or lapis lazuli bearing the same motive were found in various places and probably belonged to bracelets similar to that of King Djer. To the same sovereign belonged another bracelet consisting of 'pearls' made of gold, turquoise and amethyst, joined together by a gold thread wound round three hairs from the tail of a bull. In goldsmith's work dating from early historical times we already find one characteristic that remained constant throughout the various epochs: the craftsman's careful choice of ingenious and harmonious colour-schemes. This aesthetical ambition outweighed all commercial considerations, and it is therefore not surprising that we should find ordinary vitreous pastes set in costly gold mountings. To this must be added the study of the forms, some of which, dating from the Old Kingdom, were destined to become 'classical', while on the other hand each period had its own specific production revealing a constant search for new aesthetic notions. In the matter of personal adornment the Egyptians show that they belong to the cycle of oriental civilizations, and men therefore vied with women in the extensive use of jewels. The tombs of the earlier periods have yielded trinkets formerly used by living persons, but later, and in particular from the Middle Kingdom onwards, the goldsmiths specialized in the production of different types for the living and for the dead, since, as we shall see, a special kind of jewellery formed part of the funerary *parure*. To these categories may be added the 'temple' type, i.e. the production of ritual articles, costly statuettes of gods, ornaments for chapels, etc.

The goldsmiths also made various contributions to the work of their confrères engaged in the 'minor arts', in particular to the products of the wood-carvers who decorated furniture and the other chattels of the living and the dead.

Whereas necklaces and bracelets abound during the First Dynasty, the same cannot be said of rings, though a few gold rings have been found at Naga ed-Deir.

Various items of goldsmith's work have survived from the Second and Third Dynasties. In the interior of the 'buried' pyramid discovered in 1954 at Sakkâra by Zakaria Goneim and attributed to King Sekhem-khet of the Third Dynasty, a bracelet was found consisting of ten rows of little gold 'pearls', divided into four sections by four vertical bars of the same material. Moreover, in the corridor of the same pyramid twenty-one gold bracelets of the smooth, round type were found, as well as an interesting reproduction of the shell of a bivalve, rotating on a little pivot and presumably used for holding cos-metics. These jewels were originally enclosed in a gilded wooden casket, which in the course of time was completely destroyed, so that when the jewels were found only a few flakes of gold leaf testified to its existence.

As regards the source of the precious metal, the principal mines would seem to have been on the shores of the Red Sea and in the Nubian desert: over twenty such mines which were worked in ancient days have been discovered. Gold—the Egyptian word for which is *nub*—and negro slaves were the reasons for many military expeditions into Nubia in Old Kingdom times. The expression 'gold from Coptus' found in many texts, like that of 'wood from Byblus', suggests that gold was obtained from that area, though no traces of the metal have been found there. A possible explanation is that one of the main roads leading to the Red Sea mines passed through Coptus.

To the Fourth Dynasty belong the jewels of the mother of Cheops, Queen Hetepheres, whose tomb was found in the vicinity of the Great Pyramid. Evidence of the existence of the art of setting jewels in gold and of enchasing is provided by the hiero-glyphs incised on her litter, which we have already mentioned. Also from the Fourth Dynasty are the jewels of a princess found by Selim Hassan at Gizeh, among them a golden diadem adorned with papyrus petals and four *ibis comate*. Another necklace consists of a gold thread on which were strung fifty scarab-shaped pieces. The beetles have been identified by Keimer as the *Ægyptus notodonta latr*; they are also found during the prehistoric period and seem to have had something to do with the worship of the goddess Neith.

The specimens of goldsmith's work dating from this period confirm that it was indeed a 'golden age', in this as well as in the other arts. It was, however, centred around the Pharaoh and the members of his court, and the ornaments worn by ordinary people were cruder and simpler.

An example of applied goldsmith's work is a beautiful diorite vase with gold finishings bearing the name of the Fifth Dynasty Pharaoh Userkaf. This was found at Sakkâra and is now in the Metropolitan Museum, New York. A profusion of ornaments and of hieroglyphs with a decorative function is displayed by the 'ceremonial vase' of King Neferirkarē', likewise of the Fifth Dynasty. This is, however, in reality a contemporary copy, executed in gilded wood with incrustations of vitreous pastes, but the fine reconstruction made by the museum in Berlin suffices to show the characteristics of the original which the copy strove to imitate. Of these 'imitation' vases and their religious purpose we have already spoken when dealing with pottery. In this particular case it is interesting to note the development of the technique of inlaying gold with fillings of vitreous pastes or stones. In such work, technical and at the same time artistic, there is an obvious desire to achieve the maximum harmony of colouring and to exploit the geometrical nature of the forms, both in the individual elements of the ornamentation and in the object as a whole.

The activity of the goldsmiths resembled that of a guild, to which a far higher rank was assigned than to that of the other metal-workers. In the reign of Mycerinus, during the Fourth Dynasty, there already existed the title of 'director of the goldsmiths', and it is evident that the practise of this art brought the craftsmen into contact with nobles of the highest degree and with the sovereign himself, whose refined taste they endeavoured to please.

The art of the goldsmiths also had a share, as we have said, in the representation of divine beings. A beautiful falcon's head $9\frac{3}{4}$ inches high, dating from the Sixth Dynasty, found at Hieraconpolis and now in Cairo, is extremely expressive. Surmounted by the diadem with the double plume, its realistic character is accentuated by the eyes made of obsidian. Of the same period is the 'wide' or *uesekh* necklace of the architect Imhotep, in gold and faïence, its outer edge decorated with scarabs. This kind of necklace is typically funerary and had a decorative purpose as well as serving as an amulet. As a rule, funerary jewellery is characterized by an extreme fragility which would have made it impossible for the living to wear it and consists for the most part of elements made of faïence and vitreous pastes. This, however, does not alter the fact that, together with all the other objects that had belonged to the deceased, the jewels which he wore in his lifetime were also placed in his tomb. Had it been otherwise, the systematic spoliation of tombs that occurred during every phase of Egyptian history would have been futile, since articles made of faïence and vitreous paste would not have been an adequate reward for the trouble taken by the robbers and the dangers to which they were exposed. The 'funerary' jewels were not just utilitarian copies made in order to save money, but were produced in obedience to complex religious and magical rules governing their manufacture, their form and their use. The predominating colour, blue, which may have had something to do with Nut, the goddess of the sky, the various forms repeated time after time, the ritual application of ornaments to the mummy, were all reduced to a code during the New Kingdom, in certain 'chapters' of the text usually called 'The

Book of the Dead'. For example, Chapter CLVIII bears the title: 'Chapter of the gold necklace which must be placed round the neck of the deceased', and gives the formula which had to be spoken over this ornament on 'the day of the funeral'. The social upheaval that occurred at the end of the Sixth Dynasty involved the art of the goldsmiths to a greater extent, perhaps, than any other. With the advent of the Middle Kingdom there was a surprising renaissance, and this was the period during which Egyptian jewellery achieved its highest degree of splendour and technical perfection.

The fortunate discovery, made by De Morgan at Dahshûr, of the jewellery belonging to the princesses of the family of Amenemhet II, revealed the infinite delicacy of execution and the remarkable variety of ideas as regards form. The little crown which once adorned the brow of Princess Chnumit is a version in gold of a floral wreath and the animated interlacing of the stems is restrained by a series of cruciform clasps. The diadem of Princess Sit-Hathor-Yunut is a gold circlet studded with rosettes in a geometrical pattern, with the sacred serpent, the *uraeus*, at the front. At the back rises the 'double plume', while from three diagonal points hang forked bands, a golden imitation of ribbons. In this jewel carnelian, lapis lazuli and polychrome pastes are used in addition to gold.

The coiffures of ladies, which about this time became elaborate, comprised series of rosettes or 'buttons' of gold applied in large numbers at regular intervals.

The consolidation of the kingdom carried out by

Sesostris I and Sesostris III, together with the conquest of the Third Cataract and the fortification of the Second, resulted in a much more intense traffic with the gold-mining areas, and consequently in a wider diffusion of the metal. Silver, too, which had been so seldom used during the Old Kingdom that it was considered more 'precious' than gold, was now employed on a larger scale. During the same period several trends made their appearance in goldsmith's work: filigree work reproducing geometrical patterns, butterflies, etc., and the practice of gilding other metals by applying gold leaf.

Another typical form of jewel began to be fashionable—the 'pectoral'. This was a plaque hanging from a necklace, usually bearing a *cartouche* containing the name of the reigning sovereign, flanked by representations of the solar falcon, often superimposed on the ideogram for 'gold' and adorned with good-luck tokens such as the symbol of life (= *ankh*), and of beauty (= *nefer*), etc. Mythological motives were also found, e.g. a winged griffin crushing an enemy with its talons, and sometimes the upper edge reproduced the roof of a chapel, supported at the sides by little floral columns. Fine examples of such works have survived from Middle Kingdom days, bearing the names of Sesostris II (Plate 93) and Sesostris III, but their use soon became general and one may safely assume that each sovereign had his own. The raw materials were, naturally, gold, vitreous pastes and coloured stones. This genre was soon adopted for funerary jewellery, being made in this case of gilded wood, while in the centre the 'scarab of the heart' was often found—a very efficacious amulet against the judgement of the tribunal of Osiris. The diffusion of this kind of ornament reached its zenith under the New Kingdom, when the plaques were often made of polychrome faïence. It is evident that from the very start the 'pectoral' was considered to be both an ornament and an amulet. An analysis of its component elements leads one to suppose, in fact, that it was a question of the 'protection' afforded by the Pharaoh's name, and at the same time of the exploitation of the thaumaturgical influence of the name on the part of the wearer.

Under the Middle Kingdom ring forms became more numerous and complicated, and reproductions of the *scarabeus sacer*, in its threefold function of amulet, ornament and seal, spread rapidly. Vitrified steatite, faïence, hard stones and, more rarely, metals, were the materials in which such scarabs were executed. Many of them bear New Year's greetings, thus showing that even at that time it was the custom to exchange good wishes in a tangible form. The goldsmiths naturally paid attention to the instruments used by ladies to beautify themselves, these being enclosed in elegant caskets, with compartments for mirrors, depilatory razors, exquisite jars of alabaster, gold and obsidian for holding cosmetics and *kohl*. Mirrors, in particular, were given elaborate treatment. They were destined to 'reproduce' the beauty of the lady, and their round shape was reminiscent of the sun, the divine, life-giving star. They were consequently looked upon as magical instruments (Plate 94).

The long handles could be easily shaped like little

columns, usually of the papyriform type, and were often adorned with the head of the goddess Hathor, the patroness of love and therefore the most appropriate divinity to preside over the finishing touches when the owner was hastening to an amorous rendezvous. Gold, ebony, ivory and coloured stones were admirably suited for use in the handles, while the 'mirror' itself consisted of a highly polished circular plate of copper.

Obviously, the production of 'princely' jewellery formed a category of its own and was not, therefore, typical of the whole Egyptian people. But even the more modest classes wore graceful ornaments and the tomb of a country girl has yielded bracelets and necklaces which, though simply made, consist of amethyst, carnelian, haematite and rock-crystal.

The Hyksos invasion coincided with the Second Intermediate period and resulted in another hiatus in the art of Egyptian goldsmiths. Even when the reaction set in, it was some time before they again achieved the old standards, and the jewels of the Seventeenth Dynasty reveal a certain decline as compared with those produced under the Middle Kingdom. The diadem of a king of that dynasty, Iniotef, cannot bear comparison with the similar Twelfth Dynasty princesses' diadems found at Dahshûr. The little heads on the hilt of the sword of King Amosis of the Seventeenth Dynasty, found in the tomb of his mother at Dirâ 'Abu'n Naga, are somewhat coarsely executed. The blade has a longitudinal stripe bearing hieroglyphs, hunting scenes, and renderings of locusts, the execution being definitely inferior to that of the Fourth

Dynasty. From the same tomb came the sovereign's ceremonial axe, made of gold, ebony and electrum (Plate 95). The last-named metal was much used for ceremonial jewellery and consists of an alloy of silver and gold. The blade of the axe, attached to the handle by leather straps, has embossed patterns, quite well executed, on both sides, showing the royal *cartouches*, the king slaying an enemy, and mythical animals.

From the same source comes a gold chain made up of links, with clasps in the shape of goose-heads and a scarab of lapis lazuli as pendant. The great care given to the making of the clasps of necklaces is already revealed in Middle Kingdom jewellery, with its perfect technique of fastenings masked by elegant motives such as, for example, lovers' knots. The New Kingdom, with its policy of expansion, may well be said to represent the period of golden 'opulence'. It was in those days that a stream of gold flowed through Egypt and imposed itself as a 'fashion'. In personal jewellery this excessive abundance led to a certain decline of the forms: from the sober restraint of Twelfth Dynasty jewels we pass to Baroque *parures*, though the technique of execution still remains at a high level. Bracelets were complicated by a super-abundance of ornaments, ear-rings were developed to the point of becoming veritable architectural structures, while rings bore, among other things, elaborate and miniature-like representations of sacred boats containing divine personages.

This trend towards miniature-like detail is also revealed by the commemorative plaques in carnelian and sardonyx executed on the occasion of the jubilee of Amenophis III and Queen Tiy. But it was above all the discovery of the fabulous treasures of Tutankhamun that threw light on the various aspects of goldsmith's work during this period, providing us with a faint idea of what must have been the tombs of other sovereigns far more important than this youthful king, who died after a short reign without ever having achieved glory of any kind. Unfortunately the royal tombs in the necropolis at Thebes were despoiled to such an extent, especially those of the Twentieth Dynasty, that the tomb of Tutankhamun represents, so far, a solitary exception.

The golden 'opulence' mentioned above is here an indisputable fact: from the various sarcophagi enclosed one within the other to the mask reproducing the features of the young sovereign which rested directly on the mummy (Plate J), to the jewels, the weapons, the symbolical 'chapels'. Solid gold and thin gold leaf, pale and red gold—all of these are a real exaltation of the supremacy of this metal. The technique of the intarsia-work is perfect, and uses strips of vitreous paste, lapis lazuli and other coloured stones as if almost attempting to outvie by means of their chromatic values the mass of gold. The mask reproduces the king's features faithfully in accordance with the rules of funerary sculpture, and the same can be said of the images reproduced on the various sarcophagi. The hieroglyphic text on the golden bands is a delicate, polychrome intarsia and the attention to details is extended to the minutest particulars, such as wrapping the fingers and toes in gold leaf so as to represent the phalanges, and covering the hands with a gold cast showing them grasping the royal insignia—the sceptre and the flail. And even the sandals are covered with gold leaf and decorated with scenes showing nine enemies in bonds, who are thus trodden under foot by the sovereign: a very frequent motive, which is also reproduced on the foot-stool of one of Tutankhamun's thrones. The influence of the preceding Amarna period is shown in the figure of the king as seen on the back-rest of the throne, with its naturalistic and rather relaxed pose, as well as in certain other enchased works of somewhat inferior technical execution, but freely conceived as regards the graphical rendering. One scene shows the sovereign, seated comfortably on his stool, with a tamed wild animal by his side, shooting arrows from his bow at a group of ostriches. The queen is sitting in front of him, and with grace and naturalness offers him more arrows. The decorations on a ceremonial fan also show the king hunting, this time from a chariot drawn by prancing horses, while his faithful hound runs beside him, and behind him the symbol of life, the *ankh*, holds a similar long fan (Plate 96).

Also among the treasures of King Tutankhamun is a beautiful vase in silver with the upper edge decorated with a floral motive and a spherical body, by a goldsmith of the same period.

To the Nineteenth Dynasty belongs another fine vase from Tell Basta, inscribed with the name of Tememtaneb. It is in chased silver, incised with hunting scenes, mythical animals, etc., in two rows running round the neck. The hieroglyphic inscription, on the other hand, is placed on the upper part of the spherical body, below which the vase is ornamented with vertical rows of palm-trunks. The handle represents a gazelle in finely chased gold. This beautiful piece of goldsmith's work was found by pure chance in 1905 by a *fellah* who was riding on his donkey near the ruins of Tukh el Garmus. At a certain moment the animal stumbled against something which the rays of the sun showed clearly to be of gold. Plates, censers, necklaces, bracelets were lying all around and the *fellah*, who could hardly believe his own eyes, went nearly mad with joy. But indiscreet eyes had been watching his movements and when he returned to his village that evening the *fellah* found to his great regret that his neighbours wanted their share of the booty in return for holding their tongues. The authorities got to know of the inevitable quarrel that arose and proceeded to seize the treasure. One of the bracelets from Tell Basta bears the name of Ramesses II and in its centre portion has a curious representation of a twin-headed goose. The name of this sovereign is also found on a pectoral now in the Louvre, discovered in the sarcophagus of one of the sacred 'Apis' bulls in the Serapeum at Memphis. It is executed in gold and enamels with a symbolical representation of the 'Two Ladies', the vulture and the serpent, symbols of Upper and Lower Egypt, flanked by two *djed* or pillars sacred to Osiris, while in the curve formed by the wings of the vulture another is shown supporting the royal *cartouche*. The whole is enclosed in a frame in the shape of a *naos*, but the execution reveals a certain carelessness—harbinger of the coming decline. And in fact the jewels of Ramesses XII and Siptah, found respectively at Abydos and at Biban el Moluk, are somewhat coarse. In each case they consist of golden ear-rings: those of Ramesses XII with triple rows of pendent *uraei*, and those of Siptah decorated with striped spheres and provided with little bells. The goldsmith's art becomes more ponderous and pompous, though the raw material continues to be ever more abundant. One need only think of the period of Sheshonq, at the time of the Twenty-second Dynasty, when the total weight of gold and silver dedicated to temples was more than a ton. Various paintings on Theban tombs perpetuate the memory of 'pieces' of goldsmith's work presented as offerings. The very strange and elaborate forms show the great versatility and technique of the goldsmith-potters, and J. Vercoutter has made an elaborate study of the Aegean influence in goldsmith's work of this kind. Antelopes and gazelles provide the shapes for handles and lids, while flowers and birds are the most frequent forms of ornamentation. All this has naturally a certain Baroque flavour which is not always pleasing, but the forms of certain goblets and vases are wonderfully effective and bear witness to an art which was hardly surpassed by any other ancient people.

BRONZE

Copper was used in Egypt earlier than gold and silver. If we follow Petrie's conventional chronology we find that objects in copper occur from 'sequence date' 30–38, whereas gold and silver do not appear until 's.d.' 42. The first specimens of articles fashioned in this metal by the hands of men are thin needles, while axes, bracelets, rings, harpoons, appear, though only in small quantities, during the Negadah II period ('s.d.' 50–63). A pre-dynastic axe subjected to analysis proved to consist of 97·35 per cent pure copper, 1·28 per cent nickel and 0·005 per cent arsenic. The early historical period shows a greater diffusion of this metal in the form of axes, chisels, knives, swords, etc., but the composition is different: the analysis of a chisel showed pure copper with the addition of 2·5 per cent silver and 4·1 per cent gold. Copper does not appear to have been indigenous in Egypt and this fact has given rise to a number of theories as to the period during which it was imported and the peoples who imported it. The examination of these theories, interesting though it may be, does not come within the scope of the present work.

The first copper instruments were cast in moulds and afterwards hammered when cold, and this technique seems to have remained unchanged during the various dynastic periods. The moulds were made of steatite and serpentine and were of the open type. Primitive production would seem to have been limited to objects of everyday use, such as instruments for craftsmen, weapons and, to a smaller extent, ornaments. The water conduit of the Fifth Dynasty temple of Sahurēʿ, some four hundred yards of which have survived, was made of beaten copper without welding.

The copper basins for washing hands used in Old Kingdom days never achieved the status of 'works of art', though sometimes they have a very pleasing form.

In certain cases the specimens are covered with antimony as an imitation of silver.

The first statue executed in copper would seem to have been that of Pepy I, now in the museum at Cairo, the technique used being that of hammering over an internal body of wood, but certain parts seem to have been executed by casting on a wax model, that is to say according to the system known to sculptors as the *cire perdue* or lost wax process. Vestiges of gilding lead one to suppose that the whole statue was originally covered with gold leaf, while the crown and the royal insignia were presumably of solid gold. Copper's liability to corrode has unfortunately deprived us of any large amount of evidence as to its use in the earliest artistic productions. Combined with tin, copper provides the alloy known as bronze, which was used on a large scale in industrial production. The proportion of tin in this alloy varies from 3 to 16 per cent, and this affects both the ductibility and the colour of bronze. It is difficult to ascertain exactly when bronze began to be used in Egypt, for in Old Kingdom days copper, in a more or less pure state, seems to have been used for all those purposes for which bronze was later used. Two interesting inscriptions, which have been studied by Sethe on the Palermo Stone, mention the making in copper of a statue of the king and of two boats destined for the solar temple of Rē'. Some scenes in Old Kingdom paintings show metal-workers about to make copper basins by melting the metal with the aid of long blow-pipes. The Egyptian word for copper seems to have been *bia* and basins of various types were used as determinatives. In general the determinative is the finished bronze vase, but in the inscriptions at Wadi Maghara it is the crucible of refractory earth.

Under the Middle Kingdom the use of bronze became general and entered into the manufacture of toilet articles such as mirrors and razors, but the period of greatest development in the working of bronze was the New Kingdom. Plates, bowls and vases were cast and chased in a continuous stream and became articles of common use in the home and in temples. Many of the instruments used in ritual practices were made of bronze, among them the censers in the form of an outstretched arm with the open hand holding the little combustion chamber and terminating on the other side with the head of a falcon. These instruments, which on account of their form are called 'arms of Horus', were often beautifully executed and sometimes covered with gold foil.

But it was above all in the representation of divinities and sacred animals that the bronze-workers of the New Kingdom excelled, producing in thousands of copies the mummiform image of Osiris, the goddess Bastet in the form of a cat, Thoth in the shape of an ibis and so on for all the members of the Egyptian pantheon (Plates 97, 98, 99, 100). Such representations adorned both the houses of the living and the 'Houses of Eternity', satisfying at one and the same time both the eye and faith. The naturalistic *verismo* of the ancient Egyptians is shown in the exact, though somewhat stylized, copies they made of the original prototypes of the local fauna. The presentation of copper as the sovereign's tribute to temples reached its highest point during the New Kingdom. From the Harris papyrus we learn that over a period of thirty-one years Ramesses III distributed more than eighteen tons of copper, either raw or already fashioned, and statues and doors are not included in this figure.

At a later period a special form of purification basin made its appearance, technically known as a 'situla' (Plates 101, 102), which would seem to have been closely associated with a mythico-religious conception having some connexion with the Tree of Life, from which a cosmic goddess, usually Nut, distributed the Water of Life to the deceased. Its form is sometimes an imitation of a woman's breast, this being connected with the idea of suckling on the part of another cosmic goddess, Hathor, the 'celestial cow', with reference to the conception of the conquest of immortality and of a divine 'nourishment'. A curious situla, of the phallic type, now in the Mikhailidis collection at Cairo, bears witness to the virtue of fecundity attributed to ablutions with water from the Nile. Other 'pieces' are profusely adorned with engravings showing the deceased in the act of worshipping various divinities, while particular care was given to the bottom of the situla, often engraved in the form of a lotus.

A number of mirrors were executed entirely in bronze, with figurines of women as handles, as well as supports for vases with openwork scenes of female musicians and animals and plants, in which a certain Aegean influence is visible.

The art of bronze-working was thus essentially utilitarian and never reached the standards of decora-

tive and ornamental applications achieved by the
nobler metals. Nevertheless, the ringing sound
emitted by the sistra, the musical instruments played
by priestesses, accompanied the great temple processions, while the fumes of incense, rising from the
bronze censers, 'satisfied the hearts of the gods'.
Bronze also reflected the beauty of ladies and armed
the hands of the victorious Pharaonic warriors, immortalized the effigies of divinities and sacred animals and
propagated them throughout the world as then known
to the Egyptians. It would thus be difficult to underestimate the contribution of the industry and art of
bronze to our knowledge of the ancient Pharaonic
civilization.

CHRONOLOGY

Our knowledge of Egyptian chronology is still incomplete and as regards some periods there are notable gaps. Nevertheless, in recent years it has been enriched by valuable information contributed by archaeological research and by the application of the new method of dating known as the 'C.14 radioactive carbon method'. This was developed in particular by W. F. Libby of Chicago University and his colleagues, among them E. C. Anderson and J. R. Arnold, and is based on the possibility of measuring, with the aid of special 'Geiger counters', the radiation emanating from organic residues after appropriate treatment in the laboratory. This radiation decreases regularly from the moment when the plant, animal or human being to which the residue belongs ceases to live, and its measurement gives, with a plus or minus margin of error which is comparatively slight, the relative 'date of death'. Its application to archaeology has given results which in many cases have been corroborated by the concordance of other elements of calculation. As regards Egyptian chronology, the new system has been applied to the following cases among others: (1) Grain and corn contained in jars found in the Fayyûm, dating from the pre-dynastic period. (2) Material from the foundations of huts in the neighbourhood of el-Omari, also of the pre-dynastic period. (3) A wooden beam from the First Dynasty tomb of the Vizier Hemaka at Sakkâra. (4) An acacia-wood beam from the Third Dynasty tomb of King Zoser at Sakkâra. (5) A cypress-wood beam from the Fourth Dynasty tomb of Snefru at Mēdūm. (6) Wood from the deck of the Twelfth Dynasty funerary boat of Sesostris III. (7) Wood from a sarcophagus of the Ptolemaic era.

The chronological information obtained from the above cases is given below.

In addition to this, the Egyptian calendar, based on the heliacal rising of the brilliant star Sothis and conforming with the relative dates of the civil year, provides us with useful information. Unfortunately the elements known to us are valid only for three periods, these being the reigns of Sesostris III, Amenophis I and Tuthmosis III. These too will be mentioned in the following chronological table.

For the pre-dynastic period Sir Flinders Petrie compiled a conventional method of dating based on the evolution of ceramics as shown by the finds in bronze-age tombs. This consists of a scale of numbers known as 'sequence dates' (abbreviated to 's.d.'), No. 80 corresponding with the beginning of the historical period. The numbering originally began with No. 30 in order to leave sufficient margin for eventual new discoveries, and in fact the prehistoric station of Badari now bears the 'sequence date' 20–29.

The historical sources that can be utilized to supplement our chronological knowledge consist of original monuments belonging to various periods and of the works of writers of a later age. In particular:

1. The Palermo Stone and the Cairo Fragment, consisting of less than one-tenth of a black diorite tablet,

probably engraved during the Fifth Dynasty and listing the most important Egyptian sovereigns starting from Menes, the founder of the First Dynasty.

2. The 'Hall of the Ancestors' at Karnak, dating from the New Kingdom and now in the Louvre.

3. The Abydos Tablet, engraved by order of Sethos I on the temple walls.

4. The Sakkâra Tablet, dating from the time of Ramesses II.

5. The 'Papyrus of the Kings' in the museum at Turin. This is a document of the highest importance, but has been reduced to a very fragmentary state owing to carelessness during transport.

The above documents are called 'Royal Lists', since they consist of lists of sovereigns in the order of their succession, sometimes with the indication of the years of their reigns. To these documents can be added the works of Eratosthenes, an Alexandrian writer of the third century B.C., to whom is attributed a list of thirty Theban kings with their names transliterated into Greek, and those of Manetho, an Egyptian priest during the reign of Ptolemy II Philadelphus, who, about 280 B.C., compiled a history of his country, dividing the sovereigns from Menes to Alexander the Great into thirty dynasties, a subdivision which is still conventionally accepted. The main chapters of Egyptian history are the following: (1) Prehistoric Period; (2) Early Historical Period; (3) Old Kingdom; (4) First Intermediate Period; (5) Middle Kingdom; (6) Second Intermediate Period; (7) New Kingdom; (8) Third Intermediate Period; (9) Late (Saite-Persian) Period; (10) Graeco-Roman Period. A synthesis of these various historical periods enables us to establish the following chronological table.

I. PREHISTORIC PERIOD

This comprises the period from the first appearance of men in the Valley of the Nile to the beginning of the First Dynasty and includes the following sub-divisions:

(a) *Upper Palaeolithic*. No remains of human beings have been found, but the presence of man is proved by various 'stations', in which worked flints have been discovered. These centres are on the hills near Thebes, in the Kharga oasis, in the neighbourhood of Kéneh, at Abbāsiyeh near Cairo, etc.

(b) *Middle Palaeolithic*. The working of stone is attested in the areas mentioned above and also in the Fayyûm.

(c) *Lower Palaeolithic*. Basin of Kôm Ombo, Helwan, Wadi Angabiyeh, Fayyûm, etc. The term 'Sibilian' is derived from the locality of Sibil.

It is impossible to establish dates for this period. The inhabitants seemed to have devoted themselves exclusively to hunting and there are no certain proofs of any artistic activity. It might be possible to attribute to the *Lower Palaeolithic* or *Mesolithic* era the rock inscriptions found by Prince Kemal ed-Din, Schweinfurth and Frobenius in the massif of Ouénat, at Aswân and in southern Cyrenaica, but it is impossible to assign these with certainty to any determined epoch.

(d) *Neolithic. Northern Egypt:* Fayyûm (known as 'A'), in the stations at Kôm Washim, Dimai, etc.;

Western Delta: Merimdeh Beni Salâmeh; *Civilization of Helwan:* stations at el-Omari. The radio-carbon examination of grain and corn belonging to the 'Fayyûm A' civilization gives the figure of 6391 years with a margin of ± 180 years and for the 'hut foundations' at el-Omari 5256 ± 230 years; *Southern Egypt:* civilization of Deir Tâsa, whence the name 'Tâsian', station at Mustagiddeh, etc. On the basis of these divisions and the names of the most important stations, the civilization of Lower Egypt at this time is known as 'Merimdian' and that of Upper Egypt as 'Tâsian'.

(*e*) *Bronze Age.* Type 'Fayyûm B' with stations at Dimai, Khasmet ed-Dib, etc., this being the civilization that developed in the North, while in the South we have the civilization known as 'Badarian' from the locality of el-Badari, with other stations at Hemamiyeh and in Nubia. Copper is found together with the stone industry.

The social organization of this period comprises dwellings grouped to form villages and witnessed the transition from hunting to agriculture. The 'Badarian' civilization comprises the period of 'sequence dates' 20–29 and is followed by the Negadah civilization, also known as 'pre-dynastic', which has been studied in particular by Petrie and Quibell. This in turn comprises various subdivisions, which, however, are of no particular interest for us. Other centres of this civilization in Upper Egypt are Hieraconpolis, Tukh and Deir el-Ballâs, all to the north of Edfu, Diospolis Parva, Naga ed-Deir, el-Amrah (Amrahtian civilization), Abusir el-Melek, Tura, etc. In Lower Egypt, especially at el-Ma'âdy near Cairo.

From the point of view of the arts, the bronze age period presents a vast gamut of painting on vases with geometrical motives—from 's.d.' 40 onwards—boats, animals, etc. There are also proofs of a primitive art of sculpture, undoubtedly influenced by magical conceptions, with little human figures in clay and ivory, as well as a profusion of ornaments such as bracelets and necklaces and the existence of blue enamel. Mention may here be made of the tomb paintings found at Hieraconpolis.

During the pre-dynastic period Egypt was divided into small States which at a given moment combined to form the monarchies of Upper and Lower Egypt, the former characterized by, among other things, the 'white' crown and the latter by the 'red' crown. The unification of these two kingdoms marked the beginning of the historical period and the credit for this achievement is given to Menes, founder of the First Dynasty.

2. EARLY HISTORICAL PERIOD
(3200–2780 B.C.)

Comprises the first two dynasties and is known as the 'Thinite' period, from Thinis, the capital at that time. The royal necropolises were at Sakkâra and Abydos.

First Dynasty (3200–2980 B.C.). The radio-carbon analysis made in the tomb of the Vizier Hemaka, a contemporary of King Udimu, fifth sovereign of this dynasty, gives a date of 4883 years with a margin of ± 200, i.e. 2930 (± 200) B.C., thus confirming the chronological validity of the dates referring to the beginnings of Egyptian civilization.

Second Dynasty (2980–2780 B.C.). Existence of sculptural art proved by funerary statues and bas-reliefs, among them the stelae found at Helwan by Zaki Saad. Vases in alabaster, basalt, diorite, etc., well executed. This is a period of preparation for the following epoch and elements typical of prehistoric days, such as human sacrifices on the occasion of the death of the sovereign, gradually disappear.

3. OLD KINGDOM (2780–2280 B.C.)
Capital Memphis (Gizeh, Sakkâra)

Third Dynasty (2780–2680 B.C.). Period of great splendour in the arts. Construction of the step pyramids at Sakkâra by Imhotep, architect to King Zoser. The dating given by radio-carbon tests oscillates between 4234 ± 600 and 3991 ± 500, i.e. about 2800 B.C. The high quality achieved by sculpture at this time is proved by the statue of King Zoser. Transition from primitive architecture in clay and wood to stone buildings, for which the limestone from the quarries at Tura was used. To the same dynasty belongs another stepped pyramid discovered at Sakkâra by Zakaria Goneim, containing an empty sarcophagus in alabaster, various items of pottery and seals for jars bearing the name of a sovereign hitherto unknown: Sekhemkhet, who can perhaps be identified with the Semerkhet of the inscriptions at Wadi Maghara.

The pottery of this period presents a large variety of

forms and materials used. Among the most beautiful are the alabaster items found in the corridors inside the pyramid of Zoser. The art of bas-relief also reached its maturity. Blue faïence (produced by the melting of siliceous sand in the presence of cupric minerals) was used to decorate the walls of the royal tomb.

Fourth Dynasty (2680–2560 B.C.). Construction of the great pyramids. Snefru, founder of the dynasty, had his pyramid, of the 'rhomboid' type, built at Dahshûr. The figure given by radio-carbon tests in the tomb of this sovereign at Mēdūm is 4802 $\pm$ 210, i.e. about 2640 B.C. The art of polychrome bas-relief is perfected. Snefru's successor, Khufu (Cheops), had the 'Great Pyramid' built at Gizeh, using the local limestone quarries for the internal blocks and those at Tura for the outer casing. Other pyramids were built by the subsequent monarchs Khafrē' (Chephren) and Menkaurē' (Mycerinus). Interesting mural paintings at Mēdūm. Elegant jewellery.

Fifth Dynasty (2560–2420 B.C.). This and the preceding dynasty represent the 'golden age' of Pharaonic art. Superb sculpture, as exemplified by the 'head of a sovereign' found recently (May 1957) at Abusir by the Swiss-German Archaeological Mission. The sovereigns of this dynasty also had their pyramids, while Niuserrē' erected a solar temple which included a huge obelisk.

The last king of the dynasty, Unis, built his pyramid at Sakkâra. The remains of the 'sacred way', connecting the funerary temple of this pyramid with the valley temple, have recently been brought to light and have yielded authentic works of art and interesting historical evidence. The oldest literary compositions on religious and magical subjects are engraved on the walls of the inner chambers of this pyramid and have been given the name of 'Pyramid Texts'.

Sixth Dynasty (2420–2280 B.C.). Marks the end of the Old Kingdom. Pepy II (Phiops in Manetho's 'list') reigned for approximately a century, but during this period the germs of a social upheaval matured and eventually exploded in a revolution. Art shows signs of decadence.

4. FIRST INTERMEDIATE PERIOD (2280–2052 B.C.)

Comprises the obscure period of social and political strife, about which we have very little direct information. Struggle for power between various popular leaders; pseudo-dynasties arose (according to Manetho, seventy in seventy days). The *Seventh Dynasty* (2280) was a period of 'interregnum'. The *Eighth Dynasty* covered the years from 2280 to 2242 B.C., the *Ninth* those from 2242 to 2133 B.C., the *Tenth* those from 2133 to 2052 B.C. It is impossible to speak of any art during this period. The political centre was Heracleopolis.

5. MIDDLE KINGDOM (2134–1778 B.C.)

Reconstitution of the Pharaonic State by the princes of Thebes.

Eleventh Dynasty. First Theban Epoch (2134–1991 B.C.). The art of sculpture still reveals the effects of the revolution. Rather coarse and heavy forms during the first period, e.g. in the statue of King Montuhotep.

Twelfth Dynasty (1991–1778 B.C.). Royal residences and necropolises at el-Lisht, Dahshûr and in the Fayyûm. Zenith of the art of jewellery. Wall paintings at Beni-Hasan with flowing lines. The dating of the reign of Sesostris III according to the heliacal rising of Sothis comprises the years 1882 to 1879 B.C., while radio-carbon tests made on this sovereign's funerary boat give an average of 3621 ± 180, which in substance confirms the above dates.

6. SECOND INTERMEDIATE PERIOD
(1778–1567 B.C.)

Thirteenth Dynasty (1778–1625 B.C.).

Fourteenth Dynasty (1625–1594 B.C.). Decadence of the State organization, disruption of the constituted powers and gradual invasion of Egypt by the Hyksos, nomads of Semitic origin.

Fifteenth Dynasty (1675–1567 B.C.). Capital: Avaris (Tanis).

Sixteenth Dynasty (1660–1600 B.C.). Continuation of the Hyksos domination. The invaders adopt many of the Egyptian customs and artistic ideas, among them sphinxes, scarabs, etc.

Seventeenth Dynasty (1600–1567 B.C.). Liberation of the country from the foreign yoke by Amosis I, founder of the following dynasty. The arts are deeply influenced by the period of upheaval.

7. NEW KINGDOM (1567–1085 B.C.)

Eighteenth Dynasty (1567–1320 B.C.). Second Theban Epoch. Capital: Thebes. Great activity in architecture: temple of Queen Hatshepsut at Deir el-Bahri. The concordance of the heliacal rising of Sothis informs us that the ninth year of the reign of Amenophis I lay between 1550 and 1547 B.C., and that the years 1474 to 1471 B.C. fell in the reign of Tuthmosis III. Development of temple architecture in the neighbourhood of Thebes (Luxor, Karnak) concentrated on the figure of the local god Amun-Rē'. The son of Amenophis III rebelled against this cult and exalted that of 'Aten', i.e. the solar disc. He changed his name from Amenophis IV to Akhenaten and founded a new capital at Tell el-Amarna. The figurative arts were transformed by new revolutionary dictates of a crudely 'veristic' nature. On the death of this sovereign the priests of Amun regained power and one of the direct successors of the heretical king, in deference to the new state of affairs, changed his name from Tutankhaten to Tutankhamun. Elaborate golden jewellery.

Nineteenth Dynasty (1320–1200 B.C.). Royal residence: Raamses (Tanis), while Thebes remained the religious centre. Activity in the building of temples by various sovereigns, Ramesses I, Sethos I, etc. Royal necropolis in the 'Valley of Kings' near Thebes.

Twentieth Dynasty (1200–1085 B.C.). Reigns of the various Ramesses (III–XI). The New Kingdom was Egypt's period of maximum imperial expansion.

8. THIRD INTERMEDIATE PERIOD
(1085–656 B.C.)

Twenty-first Dynasty (1085–950 B.C.). The high priests of Amun at Thebes ascend the throne. Residence: Tanis. Collapse of the frontiers of the kingdom and decadence in the arts. The plundering of royal tombs at Thebes by robbers continues, with the connivance of the local authorities.

Twenty-second Dynasty (950–730 B.C.). The Libyans rise to power. Residences: Bubastis and Tanis.

Twenty-third Dynasty (817–730 B.C.).

Twenty-fourth Dynasty (730–715 B.C.). Disintegration of the kingdom.

Twenty-fifth Dynasty (751–656 B.C.). Ethiopian sovereigns rule Egypt from Napata (Gebel Barkal, Sudan). Signs of a renaissance in the arts.

9. LATE (SAITE-PERSIAN) PERIOD
(663–332 B.C.)

Twenty-sixth Dynasty (663–525 B.C.). Residences: Sais and Memphis, where artistic activity developed, drawing its inspiration from the old 'canons', and is known from its places of origin as 'Saite' and 'Neo-Memphis' art.

Twenty-seventh Dynasty (525–404 B.C.). Egypt is conquered by the Persians under Cambyses.

Twenty-eighth Dynasty (404–398 B.C.). Residence: Sais.

Twenty-ninth Dynasty (398–378 B.C.). Residence: Mendes. Period of small local sovereignties.

Thirtieth Dynasty (378–341 B.C.). Influence of the priests of Sais brings Nectanebus I to the throne. He restores many temples that had fallen into decay and builds new ones (Sammanud and Behbeit). Short-lived renewal of Persian domination (341–332 B.C.) effected by Artaxerxes-Ochus. In 332 B.C. Egypt was conquered by Alexander the Great.

10. GREEK (PTOLEMAIC) AND ROMAN PERIOD (332–30 B.C.)

Foundation of the city of Alexandria and reigns of the various Ptolemies. Radio-carbon test made on a sarcophagus of this period gives an average figure of 2190 years, i.e. about 340 B.C. Artistic activity strongly influenced by Greek art and products are consequently spurious. The occupying peoples adopt many Egyptian customs and usages. The Egyptian priest Manetho writes the history of his country. After the battle of Actium (30 B.C.) Egypt becomes a Roman province. Rapid spread of Christianity during the second century A.D.; Christianity in Egypt represented by the Copts, whose language is the last stage of that of the Pharaonic era. Art is inevitably influenced by this syncretism.

BIBLIOGRAPHY

The aim of the following Bibliography, which is necessarily limited, is to give the reader useful hints for a more thorough study of the various questions dealt with in the present volume.

We have also included certain articles published in specialized periodicals. The abbreviations used in such cases are the following:

ASAE: Annales du Service des Antiquités d'Égypte, Cairo.

BIE: Bulletin de l'Institut d'Égypte, Cairo.

BIFAO: Bulletin de l'Institut Français d'Archéologie Orientale, Cairo.

Catal. Cairo: Catalogue Général du Musée du Caire.

JAOS: Journal of the American Oriental Society, New Haven, U.S.A.

JEA: Journal of Egyptian Archaeology, London.

MIFAO: Mémoires de l'Institut Français d'Archéologie Orientale, Cairo.

SBA: Proceedings of the Society of Biblical Archaeology, London.

ZÄS: Zeitschrift für ägyptische Sprache und Altertumskunde, Leipzig.

ART HISTORY

ALFRED C., *Old Kingdom Art in Ancient Egypt, Middle Kingdom Art in Ancient Egypt, New Kingdom Art in Ancient Egypt*, London, 1949, 1950, 1951, 3 vols.

BÉNÉDITE, G., *L'Art égyptien dans ses lignes générales*, Paris, 1923.

BISSING, F. VON, *Der Anteil der ägyptischen Kunst am Kunstleben der Völker*, Munich, 1912.

BISSING, F. VON, *Die Kunst der alten Ägypter*, Leipzig, 1911.

BISSING, F. VON, *Ägyptische Kunstgeschichte . . .* , Berlin, 1934–35.

BOREUX, C., *L'art égyptien*, Paris, 1926.

BRUNNER, H., *Ägyptische Kunst*, Munich, 1937.

CAPART, J., *Les débuts de l'art en Égypte*, Brussels, 1904: Eng. trans. A. S. Griffith, *Primitive Art in Egypt*, 1905.

CAPART, J., *L'art égyptien. Choix de Documents*, Brussels, 1909–47, 4 vols.

CAPART, J., *Documents pour servir à l'étude de l'art égyptien*, Paris, 1927–31, 2 vols.

CAPART, J., *Propos sur l'Art égyptien*, Brussels, 1931.

CAPART, J., *Pour faire aimer l'art égyptien*, Brussels, 1949.

CURTIUS, L., *Die antike Kunst*, Berlin, 1923.

DARESSY, G., 'L'art tanite', *ASAE*, 1917, vol. 22.

DESROCHES-NOBLECOURT, C., *Le Style égyptien*, Paris, 1946.

DONADONI, S., 'Introduzione all'arte saita', in *La Critica d'Arte*, Florence, 1937.

DONADONI, S., *Arte Egizia*, Turin, 1955.

DRIOTON, E., Introduction to: *Temples et Trésors de l'Égypte*, published by Art et Style, Paris, 1951: Eng. edition, edited by R. Lang, *Temples and Treasures of Egypt*, 1954.

FRANKFORT, H., 'On Egyptian Art', *JEA*, 1932, vol. 18.

GALASSI, G., 'Dall'antico Egitto ai bassi tempi', in *L'Arte*, Rome, 1915, 18th year.

GALVANO, A., *L'Arte egiziana antica*, Florence, 1938.

HALL, H. R. H., *The Art of Early Egypt and Babylonia*, Cambridge, 1923, vol. 1.

HAMANN, R., *Ägyptische Kunst*, Berlin, 1944.

HAYES, W. C., *The Scepter of Egypt*, New York, 1953.

HERMANN, A., 'Zur Anonymität der ägyptischen Kunst', Berlin, 1936, in *Mitteilungen des Inst. für Ägypt. Altertumsk.*, Berlin.

HERMANN, A., and Wolf, S., *Ägyptische Kleinkunst*, Breslau, 1926.

KEES, H., *Studien zur ägyptischen Provinzialkunst*, Leipzig, 1921.

KEES, H., *Ägyptische Kunst*, Breslau, 1926.

KLEBS, L. S., *Die Reliefs und Malereien des neuen Reiches*, Heidelberger Akademie der Wissenschaften, 1934, Part I.

LANGE, K., *Ägyptische Kunst*, Zürich-Berlin, 1939.

LANGE, K., and HIRMER, M., *Egypt*, London, 1955.

LEFÉBURE, E., 'L'art égyptien', *BIE*, 1884, No. 4.

MASPERO, G., *Histoire générale de l'Art. L'Égypte*, Paris, 1911.

MASPERO, G., *Essais sur l'Art égyptien*, Paris, 1912: Eng. trans. Elizabeth Lee, *Egyptian Art: Studies*, 1913.

NAVILLE, E. H., 'L'art égyptien', *Annales Musée Guimet*, Paris, 1908.

PERROT, G., and CHIPIEZ, C., 'Histoire de l'Art dans l'Antiquité', *L'Égypte*, Paris, 1882, vol. I.

RANKE, H., *The Art of Ancient Egypt. Architecture, Sculpture, Painting, Applied Art*, Vienna-London. No date.

RANKE, H., Introduction to: *The Art of Ancient Egypt. Architecture, Sculpture, Painting, Applied Art*, Phaidon Press, Vienna, 1936.

RANKE, H., *Meisterwerke der ägyptischen Kunst*, Basle, 1948.

ROSS, E. D., *The Art of Egypt through the Ages*, London, 1921.

SCHÄFER, H., and ANDRAE, W., *Die Kunst des Alten Orients*, Berlin, 1925.

SCHÄFER, H., *Von ägyptischer Kunst . . .* , Leipzig, 1930.

SCHARFF, A., *Typus und Persönlichkeit in der ägyptischen Kunst*, Archiv für Kulturgeschichte, Weimar, 1939.

SPIEGELBERG, W., *Geschichte der ägyptischen Kunst*, Leipzig, 1903.

Steindorff, G., *Die Kunst der Ägypter. Bauten, Plastik, Kunstgewerbe*, Leipzig, 1928.

Stevenson Smith, W., *Egyptian Sculpture and Painting in the Old Kingdom*, Oxford, 1947.

Tel (ed.), *Encyclopédie photographique de l'Art. Les Antiquités du Musée du Louvre*, 1935.

Tel (ed.), *Encyclopédie photographique de l'Art. Le Musée du Caire*, 1947.

Worringer, W., *Ägyptische Kunst. Probleme ihrer Wertung*, Munich, 1927: Eng. trans. *Egyptian Art*, ed. Bernard Rackham, 1928.

Wreszinski, W., *Atlas zur altaegyptischen Kulturgeschichte*, Leipzig, 1923–38.

COMPARATIVE STUDIES

Frobenius, L., *Storia della Civiltà Africana*, Turin, 1953.

Groenewegen-Frankfort, H. A., *Arrest and Movement*, Chicago, 1951.

Guest, E. M., 'The Influence of Egypt on the Art of Greece', in *Ancient Egypt*, London, 1930.

Hall, H. R. H., 'The Relations of Aegean with Egyptian Art', *JEA*, 1914, vol. 1.

Kantor, H. J., *The Aegean and the Ancient Near East*, Bloomington (U.S.A.), 1947.

Vercoutter, J., *L'Égypte et le monde égéen préhéllénique*, Cairo, 1956.

ARCHITECTURE

Abu Bakr, A. M., *Excavations at Gîza*, Cairo, 1953.

Badawi, A., *Le dessin architectural chez les anciens Égyptiens*, Cairo, 1948.

BADAWI, A., *A History of Egyptian Architecture*, Cairo, 1954.

BORCHARDT, L., *Untersuchungen zur Geschichte und Altertumskunde Ägyptens*, Leipzig, 1905.

BORCHARDT, L., *Die Pyramiden*, Berlin, 1911.

BUSCHOR, E., *Bildnisstufen*, Munich, 1947.

CAPART, J., *Recueil de Monuments égyptiens*, Brussels, 1902–5, 2 vols.

CAPART, J., *L'Art égyptien*, I. *L'architecture*, Brussels, 1922.

CHOISY, A., *L'Art de bâtir chez les Égyptiens*, Paris, 1904.

CLARKE, S., and ENGELBACH, R., *Ancient Egyptian Masonry: The Building Craft*, Oxford, 1930.

DARESSY, G., 'Tracé d'une voûte datant de la III dynastie', *ASAE*, 1927, vol. 27.

DAVIES, NORMAN DE GARIS, 'An Architect's Plan from Thebes', *JEA*, 1917, vol. 4.

DAVIES, NORMAN DE GARIS, 'The Town House in Ancient Egypt', in *Metropolitan Museum Studies*, New York, 1929, vol. 1.

DRIOTON, E., 'Tombeaux égyptiens', in *Croyances et coutumes funéraires de l'ancienne Égypte*, Revue du Caire, 1943.

EDWARDS, I. E. S., *The Pyramids of Egypt*, London, 1955.

EMERY, W. B., *Excavations at Saqqara*, Cairo, 1937, seq.

ENGELBACH, R., 'An Architect's Project from Thebes', *ASAE*, 1927, vol. 27.

ERMAN, A., 'Obelisken roemischer Zeit', in *Arch. Inst. des Deutschen Reiches*, Mittheil, Rome, 1893, vol. 8.

EVERS, H. G., *Staat aus dem Stein. Denkmäler, Geschichte und Bedeutung der ägyptischen Plastik während des mittleren Reichs*, Munich, 1929, 2 vols.

FAKHRI, A., *The Bent Pyramid of Dahshûr*, Cairo, 1954.

FLETCHER, B., *A History of Architecture*, London, 1956.

FOUCART, G., 'Les conventions de l'architecture figurée en Égypte', in *Revue Archéologique*, Paris, 1896, vol. 29.

GONEIM, Z., *Die verschollene Pyramide*, Wiesbaden, 1955.

GUNN, B., 'An Architect's Diagram of the Third Dynasty', *ASAE*, 1926, vol. 26.

HASSAN, SELIM, *Excavations at Gîza*, Cairo, 1932–48, 6 vols.

HASSAN, SELIM, *Excavations at Saqqara*, Cairo, 1937.

HASSAN, SELIM, *Le Sphinx*, Cairo, 1951.

HASSAN, SELIM, *The New Pyramid of Dahshûr*, Communication No. XXIV, International Congress of Orientalists, Munich, 1957.

JÉQUIER, G., *L'architecture et la décoration dans l'ancienne Égypte*, Paris, 1922–24.

JÉQUIER, G., *Décoration égyptienne. Plafonds et frises végétales du Nouvel Empire*, Paris, 1923.

JÉQUIER, G., *Manuel d'archéologie égyptienne. Les éléments de l'architecture*, Paris, 1924.

JUNKER, H., 'Von der ägyptischen Baukunst des Alten Reiches', *ZÄS*, 1928, vol. 63.

JUNKER, H., *Gîza*, Österreichische Akademie der Wissenschaften, 1929–53, vols. I–XI.

KEESS, H., *Das Werden der ägyptischen Monumentalarchitektur*, Göttingen, 1936.

KUENTZ, C., *Obélisques*, Catal., Cairo, 1932.

LAUER, J. P., *Sakkarah. Les monuments de Zoser*, Cairo, 1939.

LAUER, J. P., *La pyramide à degrés. Compléments*, Cairo, 1939.

LAUER, J. P., *Le problème des pyramides d'Égypte*, Paris, 1948.

LEFÉBURE, E., *Rites égyptiens: construction et protection des édifices*, Paris, 1890.

MARUCCHI, O., *Gli obelischi egiziani di Roma*, Rome, 1898.

MURRAY, M. A., *Egyptian Temples*, London, 1931.

PARIBENI, R., *Architettura dell'Oriente antico*, Bergamo, 1937.

PETRIE, W. M. F., 'The Building of a Pyramid', in *Ancient Egypt*, London, 1930.

PILLET, M., 'De l'érection des obélisques', in *Chron. d'Égypte*, 1931.

PILLET, M., 'L'extraction du granit en Égypte à l'époque pharaonique', *BIFAO*, 1936, vol. 36.

PORTER, B., and MOSS, R., *Topographical Bibliography of ancient Egyptian hieroglyphic texts, reliefs and paintings*, Oxford, 1927–39, vols. 1–6.

REISNER, G. A., *The Development of the Egyptian Tomb down to the Accession of Cheops*, Cambridge, 1936.

RICKE, H., *Beiträge zur ägyptischen Bauforschung und Altertumskunde . . .*, 1939–50, Nos. 3–5.

RICKE, H., *Bemerkungen zur Baukunst des Alten Reiches*, Zürich, 1944.

SMITH, E. B., *Egyptian Architecture as a Cultural Expression*, New York, 1938.

STOCK, H., *Studien zur Geschichte und Archäologie der 13. bis 17. Dynastie*, Glückstadt, 1942.

VANDIER, J., *Manuel d'archéologie égyptienne*, Paris, 1952–55, 4 vols.

VARILLE, A., 'Un point de vue nouveau sur l'architecture pharaonique', in *Synthèses*, Brussels, No. 81. No date.

VARILLE, A., *A propos des pyramides de Snefrou*, Cairo, 1947.

WALLE, B. VAN DE, 'Obélisques d'Egypte et obélisques d'Europe' in *Chron. d'Égypte*, 1930.

WERBROUK, M., *Le temple de Hatchepsout à Deir el Bahari*, Brussels, 1949.

SCULPTURE

ANTHES, R., *Meisterwerke ägyptischer Plastik*, Stuttgart, 1947.

ANTHES, R., *Ägyptische Plastik in Meisterwerken*, Stuttgart, 1954.

ANWAR SHOUKRY, M., *Die Privatgrabstatue im Alten Reich*, Cairo, 1951.

BISSING, F. VON, *Denkmäler ägyptischer Skulptur*, Munich, 1911–14.

BISSING, F. VON, *Moderne Elemente in der ägyptischen Kunst*, Munich, 1953.

BORCHARDT, L., *Statuen und Statuetten von Königen und Privatleuten*, Catal., Cairo, 1911–36.

BOSSE, K., *Die menschliche Figur in der Rundplastik der ägyptischen Spätzeit*, Glückstadt, 1936.

BOTTI, G., and ROMANELLI, P., *Le sculture del Museo Gregoriano Egizio*, Tipografia Pol. Vaticana, 1951.

DARESSY, G., *Statues de Divinités*, Catal., Cairo, 1905–6, 2 vols.

EDGAR, C. C., *Sculptors' Studies and Unfinished Works*, Catal., Cairo, 1906.

FECHHEIMER, H., *Die Plastik der Ägypter*, Berlin, 1922.

FECHHEIMER, H., *Kleinplastik der Ägypter*, Berlin, 1922.

GALASSO, G., 'Il bassorilievo egizio', in *Critica d'Arte*, Florence, 1955, No. 10.

HORNEMANN, B., *Types of Ancient Egyptian Statuary*, Munksguard, 1951.

JUNKER, H., *Zu dem Idealbild des menschlichen Körpers in der Kunst des Alten Reiches*, Österreichische Akademie der Wissenschaften, Vienna, 1948, No. 17.

KLEBS, L., *Die Reliefs des Alten Reiches . . . Mittleren Reiches . . . Neuen Reiches*, Heidelberg, 1915, 1922, 1934, 3 vols.

LEGRAIN, G., *Statues et Statuettes de Rois et de Particuliers*, Catal., Cairo, 1906–25, 3 vols. and Index.

LEGRAIN, G., 'Introduction à l'étude de la sculpture égyptienne. Les débuts de l'art thébaine', *BIE*, 1907, No. 7.

MORANT, H. DE, 'Statuaire et frontalité dans l'art égyptien', in *Chronique d'Égypte*, Brussels, 1934.

MURRAY, M. A., *Egyptian Sculpture*, London, 1930.

SCHARFF, A., 'On the Statuary of the Old Kingdom', *JEA*, 1941, No. 26.

SENK, H., *Der Proportionskanon in der ägyptischen Rund-*

bildnerei, Archiv für Orientforschung, Berlin, 1934, vol. 9.

STEINDORFF, G., *A Royal Head from Ancient Egypt*, Washington, 1951.

TULLI, A., *Il Naoforo Vaticano*, Tipografia Polig. Vaticana, 1940.

VANDIER, J., 'Portraits de Rois', in *L'Amour de l'Art*, 1948, No. 28.

WALKER, J., *Egyptian Sculpture from the Gulbenkian Collection*, Washington, 1949.

DRAWING AND PAINTING

BAUD, M., 'Caractère du dessin égyptien', *MIFAO*, 1934, vol. 66.

BAUD, M., *Les dessins ébauchés de la Nécropole Thébaine*, Cairo, 1935.

CARLIER, A., *Souplesse et liberté dans la composition des plans égyptiens*, Académie des Beaux-Arts, Paris, 1934, No. 20.

DARESSY, G., *Textes et dessins magiques*, Catal., Cairo, 1902.

DAVIES, NINA M. DE GARIS, *Ancient Egyptian Painting*, Chicago, 1936, 3 vols.

DAVIES, NINA M., *Egyptian Paintings*, London, 1954.

DAVIES, NORMAN DE GARIS, 'An Apparent Instance of Perspectival Drawing', *JEA*, 1926, vol. 12.

DUNHAM, D., *Some Notes on Ancient Egyptian Drawing*, Museum of Fine Arts, Boston (Mass.), 1939, vol. 37.

EDGERTON, W. F., 'Two Notes on the Flying Gallop', *JAOS*, 1936, vol. 56.

FARINA, G., *La pittura egiziana*, Milan, 1929.

GLANVILLE, S. R. K., *Materials and Technique of Egyptian Painting*, Brighton, 1936.

GROFF, W., 'Note sur le rôle joué par les couleurs dans les réprésentations chez les anciens égyptiens', *BIE*, 1895, No. 5.

KEIMER, L., *Sur un certain nombre d'ostraca figurés . . . provenant de la nécropole thébaine*, Cairo, 1941.

KIELLAND, E. C., *The Human Figure. The Development from the Egyptian to the Greek way of presenting it in Painting, Drawings and Reliefs*, 1948.

KIELLAND, E. C., *Geometry in Egyptian Art*, London, 1955.

LEPSIUS, C. R., *Denkmäler aus Aegypten und Aethiopien*, Leipzig, 1897.

LHOTE, A., *Les chefs-d'œuvre de la peinture égyptienne*, Paris, 1954.

MACKAY, E., 'Proportion squares on tomb walls in the Theban Necropolis', *JEA*, 1917, vol. 4.

MEKHITARIAN, A., *La peinture égyptienne*, Skira, Geneva, 1954: Eng. trans. Stuart Gilbert, *Egyptian Painting*, 1954.

SENK, H., 'Vom perspektivischen Gehalt in der ägyptischen Flachbildnerei', *ZAS*, 1933, vol. 69.

SENK, H., 'Zum Wandel der Ausdrucksform in der ägyptischen Kunst', *ZAS*, 1936, vol. 72.

SENK, H., 'Von der Beziehung zwischen "Geradvorstelligkeit" und "perspektivischem Gehalt",' *ZAS*, 1938, vol. 74.

SENK, H., 'Zu H. Schäfers Lehre von den zwei Schichten des ägyptischen Kunstwerkes', *ZAS*, 1939, vol. 75.

STOPPELAËRE, A., 'Introduction à la peinture thébaine', in *Valeurs*, Alexandria, 1947, Nos. 7–8.

SUYS, E., *Réflexions sur la loi de frontalité*, Brussels, 1935.

VANDIER, J., *Egitto, Pitture delle tombe e dei templi*, Unesco, 1954.

VANDIER D'ABBADIE, J., *Catalogue des ostraca figurés de Deir el-Medineh*, Cairo, 1946.

WARE, E. W., 'Egyptian Artists' Signatures', in *American Journal of Semitic Languages*, Chicago, 1927, vol. 43.

WERBROUCK, M., 'Ostraca à figures', in *Bulletin des Musées Royaux d'Art et d'Histoire*, Brussels, 1932, 1934, 1939.

AKHENATEN AND THE ART OF AMARNA

DAVIES, NORMAN DE GARIS, 'Mural Paintings in the City of Akhenaten', *JEA*, 1921, vol. 7.

DRIOTON, E., 'Esthétique amarnienne', in *L'Amour de l'Art*, 1948, No. 28.

FRANKFORT, H., *The Mural Paintings of Tell el-Amarna*, London, 1929.

GHALIOUNGUI, P., 'A Medical Study of Akhenaten', *ASAE*, 1947, No. 47.

LANGE, K., *König Echnaton und die Amarna-Zeit*, Munich, 1951.

NEWTON, F. G., *Mural Paintings of Tell el-Amarna*, London, 1929.

PARIBENI, R., *Tell el-Amarna*, Bergamo, 1932.

PEET, WOOLLEY, GUNN, GUY, and NEWTON, *The City of Akhenaten*, Egyptian Exploration Society, London, 1933, vol. 1.

PENDLEBURY, FRANKFORT, and FAIRMAN, *The City of Akhenaten*, Egyptian Exploration Society, London, 1933, vol. II.

PENDLEBURY, J. D. S., *Tell el-Amarna*, London, 1935.

PENDLEBURY, J. D. S., *The City of Akhenaten*, Egyptian Exploration Society, London, 1951, vol. III.

RICKE, H., *Der Grundriss des Amarna-Wohnhauses*, Leipzig, 1932.

SCHÄFER, H., *Amarna in Religion und Kunst*, Leipzig, 1931.

Snorrason, E., 'Cranial Deformation in the Reign of Akhnaton', in *Bulletin of the History of Medicine*, Baltimore, 1946, No. 20.

Tankard, E., 'The Art of the Amarnah Period', *JEA*, 1932, vol. 18.

Weigall, A., *Le Pharaon Akh-en-Aton et son époque*, Paris, 1936.

INDUSTRIES AND MINOR ARTS

Agrasot, R., *Historia, teoria y técnica ornamental y decorativa de Egipto*, Madrid, 1909.

Burg, H., *Minor Art of Early Periods from 3000 B.C. to 1200 A.D.*, Leiden, 1939.

Carter, H., *The Tomb of Tut-ankh-Amen*, London, 1923–33, 3 vols.

Curelly, C. T., *Stone Implements*, Catal., Cairo, 1913.

Edwards, I. E. S., *A Handbook to the Egyptian Mummies and Coffins exhibited in the British Museum*, London, 1938.

Forbes, R. J., *Bibliographia Antiqua*, III–IV D: Building Materials, Pottery, Faïence, Glass, etc.; IV E–VIII: Glass, Objects and Trade, Paints, Pigments, etc., 1944–49.

Henri, E., *Décoration égyptienne*, Paris, 1923.

Hickmann, H., *La trompette dans l'Égypte ancienne*, Cairo, 1946. Cf. also the same author's articles on musical instruments in the numbers of *ASAE*.

Keimer, L., 'Egyptian Formal Bouquets', in *American Journal of Semitic Languages and Literature*, Chicago, 1925, vol. 41.

Lucas, A., *Ancient Egyptian Materials and Industries*, London, 1948.

Murray, G. W., 'Perforated Discs and Pot-Stands', in *Bulletin Inst. Fouad I*, Heliopolis, 1951.

NEWBERRY, P. E., *Egyptian Antiquities, Scarabs*, London, 1906.

PETRIE, W. M. F., *Egyptian Decorative Art*, London, 1895.

PETRIE, W. M. F., *The Arts and Crafts of Ancient Egypt*, London, 1923.

PETRIE W. M. F., *Ceremonial Slate Palettes*, London, 1953.

RACHEWILTZ, B. DE, *Scarabei dell'Antico Egitto*, Milan, 1957.

REISNER, G. A., *Amulets*, Catal., Cairo, 1907.

SACKS, C., *Die Musikinstrumente des alten Aegyptens*, Berlin, 1921.

WEIGALL, A., *Ancient Egyptian Works of Art*, London, 1914.

WILKINSON, J. G., *The Manners and Customs of the Ancient Egyptians*, London, 1878.

WOLF, W., 'Das ägyptische Kunstgewerbe', Berlin, no date, in Bosser, H. Th., *Geschichte des Kunstgewerbes*, vol. IV.

FUNERARY FIGURINES

BIRCH, S., 'On Sepulchral Figures', *ZÄS*, 1864–65.

BORCHARDT, L., 'Die Dienerstatuen aus den Gräbern des Alten Reiches', *ZÄS*, 1897, vol. 35.

BREASTED, J. H., JR., *Egyptian Servant Statues*, Bollingen Foundation, New York, 1948.

CAPART, J., 'Statuettes funéraires égyptiennes', in *Chronique d'Égypte*, 1941, No. 32; see also No. 30, 1940.

ČERNY, J., 'Le caractère des Oushebtis d'après les idées du Nouvel Empire', *BIFAO*, 1942, vol. 41.

NEWBERRY, P. E., *Funerary Statuettes and Model Sarcophagi*, Catal., Cairo, 1902–25, 2 pamphlets.

PETRIE, W. M. F., 'Funeral Figures in Egypt', in *Ancient Egypt*, London, 1916.

PETRIE, W. M. F., *Shabtis*, London, 1935.

REISNER, G. A., *Models of Ships and Boats*, Catal., Cairo, 1913.

ROE, F. G., 'The Ushabti: Its Origin and Significance', in *The Connoisseur*, London, 1915, vol. 43.

WHYTE, E. T., 'Some Remarks on the Sepulchral Figures usually called Ushabti', *SBA*, 1896, vol. 18.

WOOD-CARVING AND DOMESTIC ARTICLES

BÉNÉDITE, G., *Miroirs*, Catal., Cairo, 1907.

BÉNÉDITE, G., *Objets de toilette*, Catal., Cairo, 1911.

CAPART, J., *L'art et la parure féminine dans l'ancienne Égypte*, Brussels, 1907.

FRÉDÉRICQ, M., 'The Ointment Spoons in the Egyptian Section of the British Museum', *JEA*, 1927, vol. 13.

KEIMER, L., 'Remarques sur les "cuillers à fard" du type dit à la nageuse', *ASAE*, 1952, No. 52.

MORANT, H. DE, 'L'ébanisterie dans l'ancienne Égypte', in *La Nature*, Paris, 1938, 1st semester.

PETRIE, W. M. F., *Objects of Daily Use*, London, 1927.

PHILIPS, D. W., 'Cosmetic Spoons in the form of Swimming Girls' in *Bulletin of the Metropolitan Museum of Art*, New York, 1941, vol. 36.

RANSOM, C. L., 'Egyptian Furniture and Musical Instruments', in *Bulletin of the Metropolitan Museum of Art*, New York, 1913.

REISNER, G. A., 'The Household Furniture of Queen Hetepheres', in *Bulletin of the Museum of Fine Arts*, Boston (Mass.), 1929, vol. 27.

WENZEL, A., *Die Formen der altägyptischen Liege- und Sitzmöbel und ihre Entwicklung bis zum Ende des alten Reiches*, Heidelberg, 1939.

WHYTE, E. T., 'Ancient Egyptian Objects in Wood and Stone', *SBA*, 1902, vol. 24. See also the article by the same author under 'Bronzes'.

FAÏENCE AND VITREOUS PASTES

ARTIN, Y., 'L'antiquité du verre', *BIE*, 1894, No. 4.

BECK, H., 'Glass before 1500 B.C.', in *Ancient Egypt and the East*, London, 1934.

BISSING, F. VON, *Fayencegefässe*, Catal., Cairo, 1902.

CAPART, J., 'Verres égyptiens', in *Bulletin du Musée Royal des Arts Décoratifs et Industriels*, Brussels, 1905.

CAPART, J., 'Hippopotames en faïence', in *Bulletin des Musées Royaux d'Art et d'Histoire*, Brussels, 1939.

GAYET, A., 'Du rôle des faïences dans l'architecture égyptienne', in *Gazette des Beaux-Arts*, Paris, 1894, vol. 12.

HAYES, W. C., 'Glazed Tiles from a Palace of Ramesses II at Kautir', in *Bulletin of the Metropolitan Museum of Art*, New York, 1937.

KEIMER, L., 'Nouvelles recherches au sujet du "Potamo-geton Lucens L." ... et remarques sur l'ornamentation des hippopotames en faïence du Moyen Empire', in *Revue de l'Égypte ancienne*, Paris, 1929, vol. 2.

KEIMER, L., 'Sur quelques petits fruits en faïence émaillée datant du Moyen Empire', *BIFAO*, 1929, No. 28.

LUCAS, A., 'Glazed Ware in Egypt, India and Mesopotamia', *JEA*, 1936, vol. 22.

LUCAS, A., 'Glass Figures', *ASAE*, 1939, vol. 39.

MORANT, H. DE, 'La verrerie dans l'ancienne Égypte', in *La Nature*, Paris, 1937.

SCHLOSSER, I., *Das alte Glas*, Braunschweig, 1956.

JEWELLERY AND GOLDSMITH'S WORK

Ancient Egyptian Jewellery, A Picture Book, published by the Metropolitan Museum of Art, New York, 1940.

BATTKE, H., *Geschichte des Ringes*, Baden-Baden, 1953.

BRUNTON, G., *Lahun I, The Treasure*, London, 1920.

DRIOTON, E., 'Les bijoux à l'époque pharaonique', in *La Femme Nouvelle*, Cairo, 1947.

HALL, H. R. H., 'Egyptian Jewellery and Carvings', in *British Museum Quarterly*, London, 1928, vol. 3.

KEIMER, L., 'Pendeloques en forme d'insecte faisant partie de colliers égyptiens', *ASAE*, 1931–37, vols. 31, 32, 33, 34, 36, 37.

LORET, V., 'La turquoise chez les anciens Égyptiens', in *Kemi*, Paris, 1928, vol. 1.

PETRIE, W. M. F., *Egyptian Jewellery*, London, 1918.

ROSENBERG, M., *Aegyptische Einlage in Gold und Silber*, Frankfurt am Main, 1905.

SCHÄFER, H., *Ägyptische Goldschmiedearbeiten* . . . , Berlin, 1910.

VERNIER, E., *Bijoux et Orfèvreries*, Catal., Cairo, 1907–27, 4 pamphlets.

VERNIER, E., 'La Bijouterie et la Joaillerie égyptiennes', *MIFAO*, 1907.

VERNIER, E., 'Note sur les bagues égyptiennes', *BIFAO*, 1908, vol. 6.

VERNIER, E., 'Note sur les boucles d'oreille égyptiennes', *BIFAO*, 1911, vol. 8.

WHYTE, E. T., 'Notes on Pectorals', *SBA*, 1893, vol. 15.

WILLIAMS, C. L. R., *Gold and Silver Jewellery and Related Objects*, New York Historical Society, XI, 1924.

WINLOCK, H. E., *The Treasure of el Lahun*, New York, 1934.

POTTERY

BISSING, F. VON, *Steingefässe*, Catal., Cairo, 1904–7.

BISSING, F. VON, *Tongefässe*, Catal., Cairo, 1913.

GLANVILLE, S. R. K., 'Egyptian Theriomorphic Vessels in the British Museum', *JEA*, 1926.

JESI, F., *La ceramica egizia dalle origini al termine dell'età tinita*, Turin, 1958.

LUCAS, A., 'Black and Black-topped Pottery', *ASAE*, 1932, vol. 32.

MACRAMALLAH, R., 'Vases en pierre dure trouvés sous la pyramide à degrés', *ASAE*, 1936, vol. 36.

PEET, T. E., 'The Classification of Egyptian Pottery', *JEA*, 1933, vol. 19.

PETRIE, W. M. F., *Funeral Furniture and Stone and Metal Vases*, London, 1937.

PETRIE, W. M. F., *Corpus of Prehistoric Pottery and Palettes*, London, 1921.

QUIBELL, J. E., 'Stone Vessels from the Step Pyramid', *ASAE*, 1935.

VANDIER, J., cf. work quoted under 'Architecture'.

WALLIS, H., *Egyptian Ceramic Art*, London, 1898.

WALLIS, H., *Typical Examples of the Art of the Egyptian Potter*, London, 1900.

BRONZES

ANTHES, R., 'Technik und Datierung einiger ägyptischer Bronzen . . .', *Berliner Museen*, 59th year, 1938.

BISSING, F. VON, *Metallgefässe*, Catal., Cairo, 1901.

ENGELBACH, R., 'Seizure of Bronzes from Buto', *ASAE*, 1924, No. 24.

MOELLER, G., *Die Metallkunst der alten Ägypter*, Berlin, 1924.

ROEDER, G., 'Die Herstellung von Wachsmodellen zu ägyptischen Bronzefiguren', *ZAS*, 1933, vol. 69.

ROEDER, G., 'Komposition und Technik der ägyptischen Metallplastik', in *Jahrbuch Arch. Inst. des Deutschen Reiches*, Berlin, 1933, vol. 48.

ROEDER, G., *Ägyptische Bronzewerke*, Glückstadt, 1937.

WHYTE, E. T., 'Egyptian "Foundation Deposits" of Bronze and Wooden Model Tools', *SBA*, 1902, vol. 24.

INDEX